the big book
of kids' knits

Zoë Mellor

the big book
of kids' knits

50 designs for babies
and toddlers

hamlyn

An Hachette Livre UK Company
www.hachettelivre.co.uk

First published in Great Britain in 2007
by Hamlyn, a division of Octopus
Publishing Group Ltd
2–4 Heron Quays, London E14 4JP
www.octopusbooks.co.uk

ISBN: 978-0-600-61639-9

A CIP catalogue record for this book
is available from the British Library

Printed and bound in China

10 9 8 7 6 5 4 3 2

contents

introduction

The garments, toys and accessories in this book have been specially designed for babies, toddlers and pre-schoolers. Soft yarns have been chosen to be gentle on young skin, and the gorgeous colour schemes will grace any nursery.

In Cotton Candy you will find summer-weight projects knitted in cotton yarns – perfect for warm days or cool summer evenings. A pretty dress, cute cardigans and even a beautiful blanket are designed in fresh colours with sunshine in mind.

Wrap Up Warm will leave you feeling snug as a bug, with chunky sweaters, a comforting blanket and cosy jackets to keep the wind at bay. Ideal for days in the park kicking up fallen leaves or collecting shells on the beach.

If you're looking for something a little more adventurous, why not try some of the designs in Fun To Wear? Here you will find a Fairy Dress, Pirate Sweater and Funky Tank Top – great for parties or just adding some wow to a little one's wardrobe.

Bound to appeal to more impatient knitters, Heads, Toes & Little Hands presents beautiful designs for hats, scarves, mittens and bootees. Quick to knit and great to give as gifts, some of these projects can easily be completed in just an evening.

Nursery Comforts is bursting with ideas for toys and accessories. Ever thought of knitting your own puppet theatre? Or perhaps you'd prefer a traditional teddy bear or squishy cushion? It's all here and more.

Have fun!

yarns & colours

When creating knits for children it is important to give equal importance to the comfort of the yarns and to the allover look of the outfit. My own two children are always in my mind when I am designing and I stick to what would suit them. Children should keep their innocence for as long as possible and have fun in what they wear.

Designing for children has fewer restraints than designing for adults, as children seem happier to wear brighter shades and enjoy a sense of fun in their clothing. Be sure to take the opportunity to try out different colours from the ones I have used. You'll get a lot of satisfaction knitting up swatches while playing with colour schemes.

Colour has such a strong effect on a design – the same design can look so totally different made in a different set of shades. This is simply illustrated in the striped tank tops on page 120. Experiment with colours that catch your eye. Adding your own touches to designs will make you treasure them even more.

choosing yarn

It is a good idea to buy the yarn brand recommended in my knitting patterns. I will have chosen the yarn because its weight and texture perfectly suit that particular design. Since comfort is a top priority for kids' knits, cotton yarns feature prominently in my designs. They are soft enough for children's sensitive skin, aren't itchy and are ideal to wear all year round – warm in winter and cool in summer.

Consider the qualities of the yarn you're going to use before starting your tiny tot knit. Synthetics may be easy to wash, but natural fibres maintain their elegance for many years and get even better with age. Tiny tot knits in natural fibres can be passed down to a new sibling and still look good. Here are the pros of my favourite yarns – wool, cotton and cashmere:

wool is traditionally associated with knitting. It is springier than cotton and is warm and great for cold weather. Taking dyes well, it comes in masses of good colours. Some wool yarns, such as Botany, are softer to the touch than others, so pick them carefully.

cotton allows your skin to breathe. It is cooler than wool and non-itchy, making it ideal as an all-year-round yarn. As cotton is not as elastic as wool, maintain a fairly tight tension when knitting it up so that your knit holds its shape properly.

cotton-and-wool-mixed yarn is a great choice for children's knits. Combining the best qualities of both wool and cotton, it is warm, comfortable, non-itchy, washes well and holds its shape well.

cashmere is amazingly soft to the touch. Like wool it holds its shape well when knitted. Cashmere does have to be washed with care so it may be better used in items for special occasions. It is ideal for children with very sensitive skin.

yarn and dye lots

Yarn is dyed in batches and dye lots can vary greatly. It is essential to check the dye lot number on your yarn label to make sure that you use the same dye lot for the main colour of your knit, otherwise you run the risk of your garment being unintentionally stripy. If it is not possible to get all the yarn you need for your main colour from the same dye lot, use the odd ball for the ribbed borders. The raised texture of the ribbing disguises the colour discrepancy. For colours dotted around the design, variations in dye lots won't matter as long as they aren't touching each other.

substituting yarn

If you want to knit with different yarns from those specified in the patterns, please remember to think about the stitch size and the weight of the yarn. A yarn might knit up to the right number of stitches and rows to the centimetre (inch) but the resulting fabric may be so heavy that it pulls your design out of shape. Before you use a different yarn, I recommend that you knit a tension (gauge) square to check the stitch size and then see if you like the feel of the fabric.

colour knitting

Many of the patterns in this book involve colour knitting techniques. If the design is not a Fair Isle and the colours are in blocks, use the intarsia method of colour knitting. An example of intarsia knitting is the motif on the Pirate Sweater (see page 128). When working intarsia, do not carry the yarn across the back of the work; instead use a separate ball of yarn for each isolated area of colour. Where a block of colour is small, you can use a long length of yarn or a small amount wound around a bobbin. The intarsia method prevents the knitting from becoming too bulky and also avoids pulling and distortion across the motif. When changing from one colour to another, twist the yarns around each other to prevent holes from forming. If you still see holes at the colour-change points, try twisting the yarn twice to pull the colours even closer together.

When knitting a Fair Isle design, strand the yarns across the back of the work, picking them up and dropping them as they are needed. Make sure that you don't pull the yarns too tightly, as this will distort the shape of the knitting and make the garment narrower than it should be. The back of the Fair Isle should not have very long loops, as this type of design is repetitive and the yarn colours repeat every few stitches. If the loops are too long they can get caught and pulled by tiny fingers.

the right size for tiny tots

Knitting patterns always give the finished knitted measurement of the garment around the chest, the garment length and the sleeve seam. A good way to check that you are choosing the right size is to match these measurements to a knit that you know is just right for your tiny tot. If in doubt, pick the next size up, as the child will soon grow into it.

Once you've chosen the right size in which to knit the pattern, all you need to do is make sure your knitting turns out the way it should. Tension (gauge) is probably the most important thing to get right when beginning to knit a pattern or even to design knitwear. Many knitters get so carried away with wanting to get knitting that they don't bother to knit a test square. Please do bother – it can make the difference between a professional-looking garment and a badly fitted garment.

Tension (gauge) is simply the measurement of the tightness or looseness of the knitted fabric. On most yarn labels the recommended tension (gauge) is given in terms of the number of stitches and the number of rows over 10cm (4in) of stocking (stockinette) stitch.

Tension (gauge) determines the measurements of the garment, so if the tension (gauge) you knit to does not match that shown in the pattern, your garment will end up the wrong size. Always work to the tension (gauge) provided in your knitting pattern – designers will have knit their own swatches, which may be slightly different from the stitch size given on the yarn label. Use the needle size specified in the pattern as well, at least for your first attempt at a test swatch. Generally, the finer the yarn the smaller the needle size used for it, and the thicker the yarn the bigger the needles. I tend to use medium-weight yarns because I like to see my knitting grow quite quickly. Kids' knits are small garments anyway, so speedy results are guaranteed.

measuring tension (gauge)

To measure your tension (gauge), first knit a swatch at least 15cm (6in) square. This gives you plenty of room to accurately measure the number of stitches and rows over 10cm (4in); it can be hard to measure a smaller swatch accurately, since the edges curl up slightly. Flatten your swatch on a table top or pin it to your ironing board until it is flat. Steam press if necessary (see Blocking, page 15).

To check stitch tension (gauge), measure with a ruler and use pins to mark 10cm (4in) widthways across your swatch; always measure from the centre of your swatch. Count the number of stitches between the pins. To check row tension (gauge), do the same, but lengthways. If the number of stitches/rows is greater than that quoted in the pattern, your stitch size is too small. This can be remedied by using larger needles than stated in the pattern. If the number of stitches/rows is fewer than that quoted in the pattern, your stitch size is too big and you need to use smaller needles than stated in the pattern. Keep doing test squares, changing needle size as required, until you get the right tension (gauge).

When you actually begin to knit your garment, you may find that with more stitches on the needles you are knitting more tightly or loosely. If you think this is happening, check your tension (gauge) on the actual garment, too, and adjust the needle size if necessary.

sizing up patterns

Knitters often ask me if I can give them instructions for the next size up of a design. This is not always a quick calculation to make and I am rarely able to supply such tailor-made patterns. However, as a general rule knitters can make these amendments to my patterns themselves without too much trouble. When designing, I usually use simple shapes and set-in square sleeves which are easy to size up.

altering the length

To change the length of a garment, you need to add more rows. The pattern tension (gauge) will tell you how many rows you need for 10cm (4in). Simply divide that number by 10 to find out how many extra rows will make 1cm (or divide that number by 4 to find out how many extra rows will make an extra inch). Measure the child you are making the garment for to see how much longer you need to make it. For example, if you need to make the design 2.5cm (1in) longer, just multiply your centimetre calculation by 2.5 (or multiply your inch calculation by 1).

altering the width

Change the width of a garment in the same way that you would change the length – use the number of stitches per 10cm (4in) to calculate how many stitches to add.

a simple reminder

When altering the lengths and widths of my knitting, I find it handy to start out by jotting down the following:
1cm (or inch) up = X rows
1cm (or inch) across = X stitches

Fill in the X's with your calculations and refer back to these notes whenever you need to.

finishing your garment

Finishing your garment well is essential for achieving a successful and professional-looking garment. Although the processes involved can be time consuming, it is time well spent, for careless finishing can spoil the effect of even the most beautiful knitting.

sewing in yarn ends

The number of yarn ends left when a garment is completed can be astonishing – and daunting. Many knitters I know find the first stage in finishing – sewing in yarn ends – a tedious task. They would rather start knitting their next project than finish the job in hand. Over the years I have grown fonder of sewing in ends; it can be quite therapeutic! A quick way I have discovered is first to weave a darning needle through the back of the knitting and then thread the end through. This prevents short ends from slipping out of the needle as you weave.

mattress stitch

Sewing perfect seams is very important. Mattress stitch is the most basic seaming technique. I use it probably more than any other method as it produces a totally invisible and straight seam. It is especially useful when seaming a striped garment. If backstitch is used, which entails pinning the pieces together with right sides facing, stripes can move out of alignment, whereas mattress stitch, which avoids pinning and is worked on the right side, will achieve a perfect match.

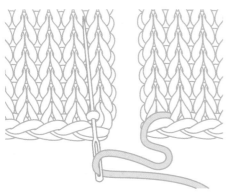

1 With the right sides facing you, insert your blunt-ended sewing needle into the knitting between the first and second stitches on the first row of the seam.

2 Then insert the needle in the other piece, in the centre of the second stitch in from the edge. Link the sides in a zigzag manner as shown above.

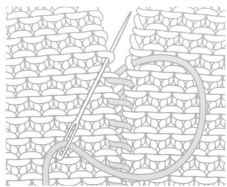

3 On garter stitch, work through the lower loop on one edge, then through the upper loop of the corresponding stitch on the other edge.

backstitch

Backstitch is good for sewing in sleeves or for tidying edges with lots of colour joins.

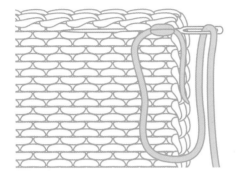 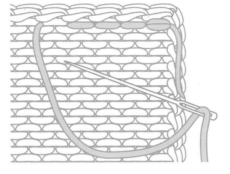

1 With right sides together, secure the seam with a starting stitch. Bring the sewing needle through both pieces of knitting, making your first stitch about 1cm (⅜in) in size.

2 Then loop back to where the yarn came out of your stitch and bring the needle out a little past the end of the last stitch. Continue like this, taking the needle backward and forward with each stitch.

blocking

Blocking, or pressing, your pieces of knitting before sewing the seams gives a more professional finish, as the edges will be flatter and not curl up. Always check the yarn label for temperatures and to see if you can press directly onto your knitting. Most of the yarns I have chosen can be pressed, but if your yarn contains acrylic it may not be suitable for pressing.

To block your knitting, carefully pin each piece face down on a flat surface – I find the ironing board ideal. While pinning the pieces, gently nudge them into the desired shape without pulling the stitches too tightly. Then lightly press or steam the knitted fabric (on the back of the work) until it is flat. If you steam your knitting, remember to let it dry out completely before removing the pins.

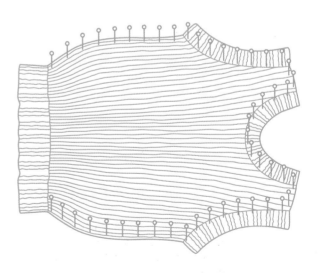

edgings and buttons

The simpler the shape and design of the garment the more perfect your finishing touches have to be. I love simple contrasting edges that give the garment that little special detail. Even simply casting on or casting (binding) off with a contrasting colour can create a surprisingly effective border. It can also highlight the motif or another element of the design. Contrasting edges feature on the Strawberries & Cream Sweater on page 64, the Heart-motif Cardigan on page 70 and the Ship-ahoy! Sweater on page 82.

Once your knitted garment is blocked and stitched together, you are ready to sew on the buttons if there are any. Choose interesting buttons for the perfect personal touch, but try not to let them take your design over – sometimes 'less is more'. Usually, the simpler the design the more detailed the buttons can be, and the more complicated the knitted fabric the simpler the buttons should be. Take your finished knitting with you when buying your buttons so you can test the effect different buttons have on the garment.

cotton candy

daisy dress

This simple flower-motif dress is really beautiful. Knitted in cotton, it is cool and comfortable and great for those hot summer days.

materials

3(4:4:5) 50g/1¾oz balls of Jaeger *Siena* in main colour **M** (turquoise/Borage 424 or mauve/Lavender 404) and one ball each in **A** (hot pink/Petunia 423) and **B** (red/Chilli 425 or white/White 401)
Pair each of 2¾mm(US 2) and 3mm(US 3) knitting needles

sizes

to fit

6–12 mths	1–2	2–3	3–4	yrs

actual measurements

chest (underarm)

53	58	62	68	cm
20¾	22¾	24½	26¾	in

length to shoulder

37	43	45	47	cm
14½	17	17¾	18½	in

tension/gauge

29 sts and 38 rows to 10cm/4in over st-st using 3mm(US 3) needles

abbreviations

alt alternate; **beg** beginning; **cm** centimetre(s): **cont** continu(e)(ing); **dec** decrease; **foll** follow(s)(ing); **in** inch(es); **k** knit; **p** purl; **rem** remaining; **rep** repeat; **RS** right side; **sl** slip; **ssk** sl 1 knitwise, sl 1 knitwise, insert tip of left needle into fronts of 2 slipped sts and k2tog tbl; **st(s)** stitch(es); **st-st** stocking/stockinette stitch; **tbl** through back of loop(s); **tog** together; **WS** wrong side

back

With 2¾mm(US 2) needles and A, cast on 119(123:129:135) sts.

Work 3cm/1¼in in garter st (knit every row).
Change to 3mm(US 3) needles and M.
Beg with a RS (k) row, work 4 rows in st-st, so ending with a WS (p) row.
Next row (RS) K3, ssk, k to last 5 sts, k2tog, k3.
Cont in st-st, work 3(3:5:5) rows.
Rep last 4(4:6:6) rows 20(18:18:17) times more. 77(85:91:99) sts.
Cont straight until work measures 28(34:35:37)cm/11(13¼:13¾:14½)in from cast-on edge, ending with a WS row.

shape armholes

Cast/bind off 5(6:6:6) sts at beg of next 2 rows. 67(73:79:87) sts.
Next row (RS) K1, ssk, k to last 3 sts, k2tog, k1.
Next row (WS) P1, p2tog, p to last 3 sts, p2tog tbl, p1.
Rep last 2 rows 2(3:3:4) times more. 55(57:63:67) sts.
Cont straight for 24(22:26:24) rows, so ending with a WS row.

shape back neck

Next row (RS) K19(20:21:23) sts, turn and cont on these sts only, leaving rem sts on a spare needle.
**Cast/bind off 3 sts at beg (neck edge) of next row and 2 sts at beg of foll alt row.
Work 1 row.
Dec 1 st at beg of next row.
Cast/bind off rem 13(14:15:17) sts.
With RS facing, slip 17(17:21:21) sts at centre back onto a holder, rejoin yarn to rem sts and k to end.
Work 1 row.
Complete to match first side from **.

front

Work as for Back until Front measures 20(26:27:29)cm/7¾(10:10½:11¼)in from cast-on edge, ending with a WS row.
Place first row of chart centrally on next row and work all 27 rows in st-st from chart **and at the same time** cont to shape sides as for Back.
When chart and side shaping have been worked,

cont straight in st-st until front matches Back to armhole, ending with a WS row.

Shape armholes

Cast/bind off 5(6:6:6) sts at beg of next 2 rows. 67(73:79:87) sts.

Next row (RS) K1, ssk, k to last 3 sts, k2tog, k1.

Next row (WS) P1, p2tog, p to last 3 sts, p2tog tbl, p1.

Rep last 2 rows 2(3:3:4) times more, so ending with a WS row. 55(57:63:67) sts.

Shape front neck

Next row (RS) K22(23:25:27) sts, turn and cont on these sts only, leaving rem sts on a spare needle.

**Cast/bind off 2 sts at beg (neck edge) of next and foll alt row, then dec 1 st at beg of foll 5(5:6:6) alt rows. 13(14:15:17) sts.

Cont straight for 16(14:16:14) rows more.

Cast/bind off.

With RS facing, slip 11(11:13:13) sts at centre front onto a holder, rejoin yarn to rem sts and k to end.

Work 1 row.

Complete to match first side from **.

neck edging

Join right shoulder.

With RS facing, 2¾mm(US 2) needles and A, pick up and k 32(32:34:34) sts down left front neck, k across 11(11:13:13) sts at centre front, pick up and k 32(32:34:34) sts up right front neck, 9 sts down right back neck, k across 17(17:21:21) sts at centre back, then pick up and k 9 sts up left back neck. 110(110:120:120) sts.

K 2 rows.

Cast/bind off knitwise.

armhole edging

Join left shoulder and neck edge seam.

With RS facing, 2¾mm(US 2) needles and A, pick up and k 82(82:92:92) sts around armhole edge.

K 2 rows.

Cast/bind off knitwise.

to finish

Join side and armhole edge seams.

flower chart

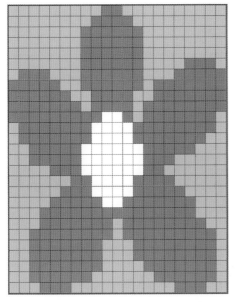

key

 A

M

 B

little star sweater

Green and turquoise is a great colour combination for both girls and boys. The 'little star' in your life will love the striped arms and star on this sweater.

materials

3(3:4:4) 50g/1¾oz balls of Rowan *Cotton Glacé* in main colour **M** (turquoise/Pier 809) and one ball each in **A** (light green/Bud 800) and **B** (off-white/Ecru 725)
Pair of 3¾mm(US 5) knitting needles

sizes

to fit

6–12 mths	1–2	2–3	3–4	yrs
actual measurements				
chest				
56	61	66	71	cm
22	24	26	28	in
length				
30	33	36	38	cm
11¾	13	14	15	in
sleeve seam				
18	21	23	28	cm
7	8¼	9	11	in

tension/gauge

23 sts and 32 rows to 10cm/4in over st-st using 3¾mm(US 5) needles

abbreviations

alt alternate; **beg** beginning; **cm** centimetre(s); **cont** continu(e)(ing); **dec** decrease; **foll** follow(s)(ing); **in** inch(es); **inc** increase; **k** knit; **p** purl; **patt** pattern; **rem** remaining **rep** repeat **RS** right side; **st(s)** stitch(es) **st-st** stocking/stockinette stitch; **WS** wrong side

note

When working from chart, use a separate small ball of yarn for motif, twisting yarns at colour change to avoid holes.

back

With 3¾mm(US 5) needles and M, cast on
64(70:76:82) sts.
Beg with a RS (k) row, work 5 rows in st-st.
Change to A and p 1 row.
Now work in rib as foll:
1st rib row (RS) K1(2:1:2), p2, [k2, p2] to last
1(2:1:2) sts, k1(2:1:2).
2nd rib row (WS) P1(2:1:2), k2, [p2, k2] to last
1(2:1:2) sts, p1(2:1:2).
Rep last 2 rows 4 times more.**
Change to M.
Beg with a RS (K) row, work 48(54:60:64) rows in
st-st.
shape armholes
Cont in st-st, cast/bind off 5(5:6:6) sts at beg of next
2 rows.
Cont straight for 36(40:42:46) rows more.

star chart

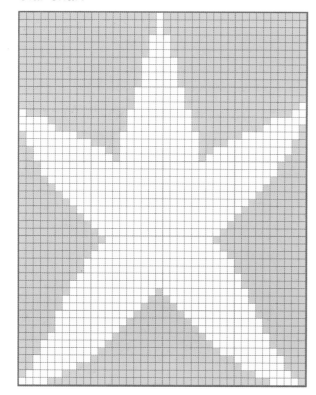

key
☐ B
▨ M

shape shoulders

Cast/bind off 8(9:9:10) sts at beg of next 2 rows
and 7(8:9:10) sts at beg of foll 2 rows.
Leave rem 24(26:28:30) sts on a holder.

front

Work as for Back to **.
Change to M.
Beg with a RS (K) row, work 18(22:26:28) rows in
st-st, so ending with a WS (p) row.
place motif
Next row (RS) K12(15:18:21)M, k across 40 sts
of first row of chart, k12(15:18:21)M.
Cont in st-st foll chart until chart row 30(32:34:36)
has been worked.
shape armholes
Keeping chart correct, cast/bind off 5(5:6:6) sts at
beg of next 2 rows.
Cont straight until all 50 chart rows have been
worked.
Work 4(8:12:16) rows more, so ending with a
WS row.
shape neck
Next row (RS) K22(25:27:30), turn and cont on
these sts only, leaving rem sts on a spare needle.
Cast/bind off 2 sts at beg (neck edge) of next and
foll alt row, then dec 1 st at beg of next 3(4:5:6) alt
rows.
Work 4(4:2:2) rows more.
shape shoulder
Cast/bind off 8(9:9:10) sts at beg of next row and
rem 7(8:9:10) sts at beg of foll alt row.
With RS facing, slip 10 sts at centre front onto a
holder, rejoin yarn to rem sts and complete to
match first side, reversing shaping.

sleeves

With 3¾mm(US 5) needles and M, cast on
36(38:38:40) sts.
Beg with a RS (k) row, work 5 rows in st-st.
Change to A and p 1 row.
Now work in rib as foll:
1st rib row (RS) K1(2:2:1), p2, [k2, p2] to last
1(2:2:1) sts, k1(2:2:1).

2nd rib row (WS) P1(2:2:1), k2, [p2, k2] to last
1(2:2:1) sts, p1(2:2:1).
Rep last 2 rows 4 times more.
Change to M.
Beg with a RS (k) row, work alternating 10-row st-st
stripes of M and C **and at the same time** inc 1 st at
each end of 3rd(3rd:5th:5th) row and every foll 4th
row until there are 60(64:68:72) sts.
Cont straight until sleeve measures
15(18:20:25)cm/6(7:7¾:9¾)in from end of ribbing.
Mark each end of last row, then work 6(6:8:8) rows
more.
Cast/bind off.

neckband
Join right shoulder seam.
With RS facing, 3¾mm (US 5) needles and A, pick up
and k 17(19:19:21) sts down left front neck, k across

10(10:12:12) sts at centre front, pick up and k
17(19:19:21) sts up right front neck, then k across
24(26:28:30) sts at centre back. 68(74:78:84) sts.
1st rib row (WS) P1(2:2:1), k2, [p2, k2] to last
1(2:2:1) sts, p1(2:2:1).
2nd rib row (RS) K1(2:2:1), p2, [k2, p2] to last
1(2:2:1) sts, k1(2:2:1).
Rep last 2 rows twice more and first rib row again.
Change to M and work 6 rows in st-st, beg with a RS
(k) row.
Cast/bind off.

to finish
Join left shoulder and neckband seam. Sew sleeves into
armholes, joining row ends above markers to cast-
/bound-off sts at underarm. Join side and sleeve
seams.

lacy sweater

Pretty without being fussy or frilly, this sweater's lacy edging picks up on the flower motif. It looks great worn with simple linen trousers.

materials

6(6:7:7) 50g/1¾oz balls of Rowan *Handknit DK Cotton* in pink/Sugar 303

Pair each of 3¾mm(US 5) and 4mm(US 6) knitting needles

sizes

to fit

6–12 mths	1–2	2–3	3–4	yrs

actual measurements

chest

56	61	66	71	cm
22	24	26	28	in

length

33	36	39	41	cm
13	14	15¼	16¼	in

sleeve seam

18	21	23	27	cm
7	8¼	9	10½	in

tension/gauge

20 sts and 28 rows to 10cm/4in over reverse st-st using 4mm(US 6) needles

abbreviations

alt alternate; **beg** beginning; **cm** centimetre(s); **cont** continu(e)(ing); **dec** decrease; **foll** follow(s)(ing); **in** inch(es); **inc** increase; **k** knit; **kfb** k into front and back of next st; **MB (make bobble)** [k1, p1, k1, p1, k1] into next st, turn, p5, turn, pass 2nd, 3rd, 4th and 5th sts over first st and k this st tbl; **p** purl; **patt** pattern; **pfb** p into front and back of next st; **psso** pass slipped st over; **rem** remaining; **rep** repeat; **RS** right side; **skpo** sl 1, k1, pass slipped st over; **sl** slip; **st(s)** stitch(es); **st-st** stocking/stockinette stitch; **tbl** through back of loops; **tog** together; **WS** wrong side; **yf (yarn forward)** bring yarn forward between needles and over right needle to make a st; **yo (yarn over needle)** take yarn over right needle to make a st; **yrn (yarn round needle)** wrap yarn around right needle from front to back and bring to front again between needles to make a st; **ytf (yarn to front)** bring yarn to front of work

stitch patterns

diagonal edging
Worked over 8 sts.
1st foundation row (RS) K6, kfb, ytf, sl 1 purlwise. 9 sts.
2nd foundation row (WS) K1tbl, k1, [yf, skpo, k1] twice, ytf, sl 1 purlwise. 9 sts.
1st row K1tbl, k to last st, kfb, turn and cast on 2 sts. 12 sts.
2nd row K1, kfb, k2, [yf, skpo, k1] twice, yf, k1, ytf, sl 1 purlwise. 14 sts.
3rd row K1tbl, k to last 2 sts, kfb, ytf, sl 1 purlwise. 15 sts.
4th row K1tbl, kfb, k2, [yf, skpo, k1] 3 times, k1, ytf, sl 1 purlwise. 16 sts.
5th row K1tbl, k to last 2 sts, k2tog. 15 sts.
6th row Sl 1 purlwise, k1, psso, skpo, k4, [yf, skpo, k1] twice, ytf, sl 1 purlwise. 13 sts.
7th row K1 tbl, k to last 2 sts, k2tog. 12 sts.
8th row Cast/bind off 3 sts, k2, yf, skpo, k1, yf, skpo, ytf, sl 1 purlwise. 9 sts.
The last 8 rows form the patt and are repeated.

flower motif
Worked on a background of reverse st-st over 15 sts.
1st row (RS) P5, k2, p1, k2, p5.
2nd row K5, p2, k1, p2, k5.
3rd row P4, k2tog, k1, yrn, p1, yo, k1, skpo, p4.
4th row K4, p3, k1, p3, k4.
5th row P3, k2tog, k1, yf, k1, p1, k1, yf, k1, skpo, p3.
6th row K3, p4, k1, p4, k3.
7th row P2, k2tog, k1, yf, k2, p1, k2, yf, k1, skpo, p2.
8th row K2, p5, k1, p5, k2.
9th row P1, k2tog, k1, yf, k3, p1, k3, yf, k1, skpo, p1.
10th row K1, [p6, k1] twice.
11th row [K2tog, k1, yf, k1] twice, yf, k1, skpo, k1, yf, k1, skpo.
12th row P6, k1, p1, k1, p6.
13th row K3, k2tog, k1, yrn, p1, k1, p1, yo, k1, skpo, k3.
14th row P5, k2, p1, k2, p5.
15th row K2, k2tog, k1, yrn, p2, k1, p2, yo, k1, skpo, k2.
16th row P4, k3, p1, k3, p4.
17th row K1, k2tog, k1, yrn, p3, k1, p3, yo, k1, skpo, k1.
18th row P3, k4, p1, k4, p3.
19th row K2tog, k1, yrn, p3, MB, p1, MB, p3, yo, k1, skpo.
20th row P1, k13, p1.
21st row P4, MB, p5, MB, p4.
22nd, 24th, 26th, 28th and 30th rows K15.
23rd row P3, MB, p1, [p2tog, yrn] twice, p2, MB, p3.
25th row P3, MB, [p2tog, yrn] 3 times, p1, MB, p3.
27th row P3, MB, p1, [p2tog, yrn] twice, p2, MB, p3.
29th row P4, MB, p5, MB, p4.
31st row P6, MB, p1, MB, p6.
These 31 rows form the flower motif.

sleeve pattern stitch
1st and 2nd rows K.
3rd row (WS) P1, [yrn, p2tog] to end.
4th–6th rows K.
7th–10th rows Beg with a WS (p) row, work 4 rows in st-st.
These 10 rows form the patt and are repeated.

back

With 4mm(US 6) needles, cast on 8 sts.
Work 2 foundation rows of diagonal edging, then work 8-row rep of edging 14(16:18:19) times, ending with an 8th row.
Cast/bind off.
With RS facing, pick up and k55(65:71:73) sts along unscalloped edge of edging.
1st row (WS) P1, pfb, p to last 3 sts, pfb, p2. 57(67:73:75) sts.
K 3 rows.
5th row (WS) P1, [yrn, p2tog] to end.
K 3 rows.**
Beg with a WS (k) row, work in reverse st-st for 27(33:41:45) rows.

shape armholes

Cont in reverse st-st, cast/bind off 3(3:4:4) sts at beg of next 2 rows. 51(61:65:67) sts.

Work 28(30:32:34) rows more in reverse st-st.

shape back neck and shoulders

Next row (RS) P18(20:21:22), turn and cont on these sts only, leaving rem sts on a spare needle.

Cast/bind off 2 sts at beg (neck edge) of next and foll alt row.

Cast/bind off rem 14(16:17:18) sts.

With RS facing, slip 15(21:23:23) sts at centre back onto a holder, rejoin yarn to rem sts and p to end.

K 1 row.

Cast/bind off 2 sts at beg (neck edge) of next and foll alt row.

Cast/bind off rem 14(16:17:18) sts.

front

Work as for Back to **.

Beg with a WS (k) row, work in reverse st-st for 15(21:31:37) rows.

place flower motif

Next row (RS) P21(26:29:30), work 15 sts of first row of flower motif, p21(26:29:30).

Next row K21(26:29:30), work 2nd row of flower motif, k21(26:29:30).

These 2 rows set position of motif.

Work 10(10:8:6) rows more as set.

shape armhole

Cont to work motif in position as set, cast/bind off 3(3:4:4) sts at beg of next 2 rows. 51(61:65:67) sts.

Work rem 17(17:19:21) motif rows.

Cont in reverse st-st, work 1(3:3:3) rows more, so ending with a WS row.

shape neck

Next row (RS) P20(24:25:26), turn and cont on these sts only, leaving rem sts on a spare needle.

***Cast/bind off 2(3:3:3) sts at beg (neck edge) of next row, 2 sts at beg of foll 1(2:2:2) alt rows and 1 st at beg of next 2(1:1:1) alt rows.

Work 6 rows.

Cast/bind off rem 14(16:17:18) sts.

With RS facing, slip 11(13:15:15) sts at centre front onto a holder, rejoin yarn to rem sts on spare needle and p to end.

K 1 row.

Complete to match first side from *** to end.

sleeves

With 4mm(US 6) needles, cast on 33(33:35:35) sts.

Work in sleeve patt st, inc 1 st at each end of every 6th and foll 4th rows alternately until there are 51(53:57:59) sts, taking all inc sts into patt.

Cont straight in patt until sleeve measures 18(21:23:27)cm/7(8¼:9:10½)in from cast-on edge.

Mark each end of last row, then work 4(4:5:5) rows more.

Cast/bind off.

neckband

Join right shoulder seam.

With RS facing and 3¾mm(US 5) needles, pick up and k 17(17:18:18) sts down left front neck, k across 11(13:15:15) sts at centre front, pick up and k 18(18:19:19) sts up right front neck and 6 sts down right back neck, k across 15(21:23:23) sts at centre back and inc 2 sts evenly for first size only, then pick up and k 6 sts up left back neck. 75(81:87:87) sts.

1st and 2nd rows K.

3rd row (WS) P1, [yrn, p2tog] to end.

4th–6th rows K.

Cast/bind off knitwise.

to finish

Join left shoulder and neckband seam. Sew sleeves into armholes, joining row ends above markers to cast-/bound-off sts at underarm. Join sleeve, side and edging seams.

1-2-3 sweater

Teach your child to count with this stripy sweater, which is ideal for a first day at nursery school. The cotton yarn makes it perfect for spring days or summer evenings.

materials

2(2:2) 50g/1¾oz balls of Rowan *Glacé* in **A** (blue/Splendour 810), 1(2:2) balls in each of **B** (turquoise/Pie 809), **C** (ecru/Ecru 725), **D** (mauve/Hyacinth 787) and **E** (yellow/Butter 795)

Pair of 3¾mm(US 5) knitting needles
Spare knitting needle
2 buttons

sizes

to fit

6–12 mths	1–2	2–3	yrs
actual measurements			
chest			
56	61	66	cm
22	24	26	in
length			
30	33	36	cm
11¾	13	14¼	in
sleeve seam			
18	21	23	cm
7	8¼	9	in

tension/gauge

23 sts and 32 rows to 10cm/4in over st-st using 3¾mm(US 5) needles

abbreviations

cm centimetre(s); **cont** continue; **foll(s)** follow(s)(ing); **in** inch(es); **inc** increas(e)(ing); **k** knit; **k2tog** knit next 2 sts together; **mm** millimetre(s); **p** purl; **PM** place markers; **rem** remain(ing); **rep** repeat(ing); **RS** right side; **st(s)** stitch(es); **st-st** stocking/stockinette stitch; **WS** wrong side; **yo (yarn over needle)** take yarn over right needle to make a st

note

When working from chart, use separate small balls of yarn for each colour area and twist yarns at colour change to avoid holes.

Beg with a k (RS) row, work 15 rows in st-st from chart for back working between lines for correct size.
Cont in st-st in stripe sequence as given until back measures 18(20:22)cm/7(7¾:8¾)in from cast-on edge, ending with a p row.
shape armholes
Cont in st-st and stripe sequence, cast/bind off 5(5:6) sts at beg of next 2 rows. 54(60:64) sts. **
Cont straight until back measures 30(33:36)cm/11¾(13:14¼)in, ending with a p row.
shape shoulders
1st row (RS) Cast/bind off 15(17:18) sts, k to end.
2nd row P15(17:18) sts, turn and cont on these sts only for shoulder button band and slip rem 24(26:28) sts onto a spare needle for back neck.
Next row (RS) K2, [p2, k2] 2(3:3) times, p2, k3(1:2).
Next row P3(1:2), [k2, p2] 3(4:4) times.
Rep the last 2 rows once more.
Cast off in rib.

front

Work as given for Back from ** to **, but work chart for front between lines for correct size.
Cont straight until 14(16:16) rows less than Back to shoulder have been worked, so ending with a p row.
shape neck
1st row (RS) K23(25:27), turn and cont on these sts only, leave rem sts on a holder.
2nd row Cast/bind off 2 sts, p to end. 21(23:25) sts.
3rd row K.
4th row Cast/bind off 2 sts, p to end. 19(21:23) sts.
5th–8th(8th:9th) rows Dec 1 st at beg of row, work to end. 15(17:18) sts.
Work 2(4:5) more rows in st-st.
buttonhole band
Next row (RS) K3(1:2), [p2, k2] 3(4:4) times.
Next row P2, [k2, p2] 2(3:3) times, k2, p3(1:2).
Next row (buttonhole row) K3(1:2), [p2, k2] 0(1:1) time, p2, k2tog, yo, [p2, k2] twice.
Next row P2, [k2, p2] 2(3:3) times, k2, p3(1:2).
Cast off in rib.
With RS facing, sl 8(10:10) sts at centre front onto a holder, rejoin yarn to rem sts from spare needle and k to end.

stripe sequence

*8 rows A, 8 rows B, 8 rows C, 8 rows D, 8 rows E, repeat from *.

back

**With 3¾mm(US 5) needles and A, cast on 64(70:76) sts.
1st row (RS) K1(2:1), p2, *k2, p2, rep from * to last 1(2:1) sts, k1(2:1).
2nd row (WS) P1(2:1), k2, *p2, k2, rep from * to last 1(2:1) sts, p1(2:1).
Rep 1st and 2nd rows 4 more times.

1st row P.
2nd row Cast/bind off 2 sts, k to end. 21(23:25) sts.
3rd row P.
4th row Cast/bind off 2 sts, k to end. 19(21:23) sts.
5th–8th(8th:9th) rows Dec 1 st at beg of row, work to end. 15(17:18) sts.
Work 6(8:8) more rows in st-st.
Cast/bind off.

sleeves

With 3¾mm(US 5) needles and A, cast on 34(34:38) sts.
1st row (RS) K2, *p2, k2, rep from * to end.
2nd row (WS) P2, *k2, p2, rep from * to end.
Rep these 2 rows 4 more times.
Beg with a k (RS) row, work 15 rows from chart between lines for correct size and garment piece, then cont in st-st in stripe sequence as before while **at the same time**, inc 1 st at each end of 3rd(3rd:3rd) row and every foll 3rd row until there are 56(60:64) sts.
Cont straight until sleeve measures 18(21:23)cm/7(8¼:9) in from cast-on edge, PM at each end of last row
Work 6(6:8) more rows.
Cast/bind off.

neckband

Join right shoulder seam.
With RS facing, 3¾mm(US 5) needles and A, pick up and k 20(22:24) sts down left front neck, k across 8(10:10) sts at centre front, pick up and k 18(20:20) sts up right front neck, then k across 24(26:28) sts at centre back. 70(76:86) sts.
1st row (WS) P2, *k2, p2, rep from * to end.
2nd row (RS) K2, *p2, k2, rep from * to end.
3rd row P2, *k2, p2, rep from * to end.
4th row (buttonhole row) K2, p2, k2tog, yo, *p2, k2, rep from * to end.
Work 3 rows in rib.
Cast/bind off in rib.

to finish

Overlap button band with buttonhole band and catch in place at armhole edge. With centre of cast/bound-edge of sleeve to shoulder, sew sleeves into armholes with row ends above markers sewn to cast/bound-off sts at underarm. Join side and sleeve seams. Sew buttons onto button band and neckband to correspond with buttonholes.

key

■ A
■ B
□ C

numbers motif

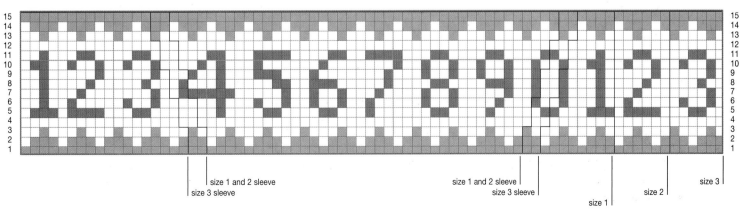

polka dot button-up

This spotted cardigan with its pretty picot edge looks equally great worn with jeans or with a favourite summer dress.

materials

4(5:5) 50g/1¾oz balls of Jaeger *Aqua Cotton* in **M** (dark pink/India 322) and 1 ball in **A** (ecru/Creme 301)
Pair each of 3mm(US2–3) and 3¾mm(US 5) needles
Safety pin
5 buttons

sizes

to fit

6–12 mths	1–2	2–3	yrs
actual measurements			
chest			
56	63	70	cm
22	24¾	27½	in
back length			
32	37	41	cm
12½	14½	16	in
wingspan			
61	76	85	cm
24	30	33½	in

tension/gauge

23 sts and 32 rows to 10cm/4in over st-st using 3¾mm(US 5) needles

abbreviations

alt alternate; **beg** begin(ning); **cm** centimetre(s); **cont** continue; **dec** decreas(e)(ing); **foll(s)** follow(s)(ing); **inc** increas(e)(ing); **in** inch(es); **k** knit; **k2tog** knit next 2 sts together; **mm** millimetre(s); **p** purl; **patt** pattern; **rem** remain(ing); **rep** repeat; **RS** right side; **st(s)** stitch(es); **st-st** stocking/stockinette stitch; **WS** wrong side; **yo (yarn over needle)** take yarn over right needle to make a st

note

When working from chart, use separate small balls of yarn for each colour area and twist yarns at colour change to avoid holes.

back

With 3¾mm(US 5) needles and M, cast on 64(72:80) sts.

Working in st-st, beg with a k row and using intarsia method, rep the 42-row patt from the chart throughout, working between the lines for correct size and garment piece.

Cont until work measures 17(21:24)cm/6¾(8¼:9½)in, ending with a p row.

shape armhole

Cast/bind off 4 sts beg next 2 rows.

Cont without shaping until back measures 30.5(35.5:39.5)cm/12(14:15½) in, ending with a p row.

Note patt row.

shape shoulders and neck

1st row Cast/bind off 8(9:11) sts, patt 11(13:14), cast/bind off 18(20:22) sts, patt to end.

Work on this last set of sts.

2nd row Cast/bind off 8(9:11) sts, patt to end.

3rd row Cast/bind off 3 sts, patt to end.

4th row Cast/bind off.

Rejoin yarn at neck edge of first set of sts and work 3rd and 4th rows.

left front

With 3¾mm(US 5) needles and M, cast on 32(36:40) sts.

Working in st-st, beg with a k row and using intarsia method, rep the 42-row patt from the chart throughout, working between the lines for correct size and garment piece.

Cont until work measures 17(21:24)cm/6¾(8¼:9½)in, ending with a p row.

Shape armhole

Cast/bind off 4 sts, patt to end

Cont without shaping until 15(15:17) rows less have been worked than noted patt row for shoulder shaping, so ending with a k row.

shape neck

1st row (WS) cast/bind off 5(6:6) sts, patt to end.

2nd–4th rows Cont in patt dec 1 st at neck edge.

5th row P.

Cont in patt dec 1 st at neck edge on next (6th) row

and foll alt rows until 16(19:22) sts rem.

Work 3 more rows.

shape shoulder

1st row (RS) Cast/bind off 8(9:11) sts, patt to end.

2nd row P.

Cast/bind off.

right front

Work as given for Left Front, reversing all shapings.

sleeves

With 3mm(US 2–3) needles and M, cast on 33(35:37) sts.

1st row *K1, p1, rep from * to last st, k1

Repeat 1st row six times more.

8th row As 1st row, inc 1 st at end of row. 34(36:38) sts.

Change to 3¾mm(US 5) needles and st-st.

Working in st-st, beg with a k row and using intarsia method, rep the 42-row patt from the chart throughout, working between the lines for correct size and garment piece, **while at the same time**, inc 1 st at each end of 3rd row and every foll 4th(6th:6th) row until 56(44:52) sts and then sizes 2 and 3 on every foll 4th row until 66(72) sts.

Cont without shaping until work measures 23(28:31)cm/9(11:12¼)in.

Cast/bind off.

PM at each end of 6th row from cast/bind off-edge.

button band

With 3mm(US 2–3) needles and M, cast on 6 sts.

1st row *K1, p1, rep from * to end.

2nd row *P1, p1, rep from * to end.

Cont in moss/seed st until band, when slightly stretched, fits from cast-on edge to neck of Left Front.

Break yarn and leave sts on safety pin.

Mark positions for 5 buttons, the first 1cm/¾in from cast-on edge, the fifth 1cm/¾in above button band in the neckband, the remaining 3 evenly spaced between.

Sew band to Right Front.

buttonhole band

Work as for Button Band, making buttonholes where marked.

Buttonhole row Moss/seed st 2 sts, k2tog, yo, moss/seed st 2 sts.

Do not break yarn.

neckband

Join shoulder seams. With RS facing, 3mm(US 2–3) needles and M, moss/seed st across buttonhole band, pick up and k 20(20:22) sts from right front neck, 24(26:28) sts from back neck, 20(20:22) sts from left front neck, then moss/seed st across button band. 76(78:84) sts.

Work 5 rows in moss/seed st, making last buttonhole in 2nd row.

edging

With 3mm(US 2–3) needles and M, cast on 2 sts.

1st row Inc in 1st st, k1. 3 sts.
2nd row K1, p1, inc in last st. 4 sts.
3rd row Inc in 1st st, k1, p1, k1. 5 sts.
4th row [K1, p1] twice, inc in last st. 6 sts.
5th row Moss/seed st without shaping.
6th–9th rows Moss/seed st, dec 1 st at shaped edge on every row. 2 sts.
10th row K2.

Rep 1st–10th rows until straight edge fits lower edge of garment, excluding front bands, finishing with a 9th row before cast/bind off.

to finish

With centre cast/bound-off edge of sleeve to shoulder, sew sleeves into armholes with row ends above markers sewn to cast/bound-off sts at underarm. Join side and sleeve seams. Sew on buttons to correspond with buttonholes.

key

 M
□ A

polka dot chart

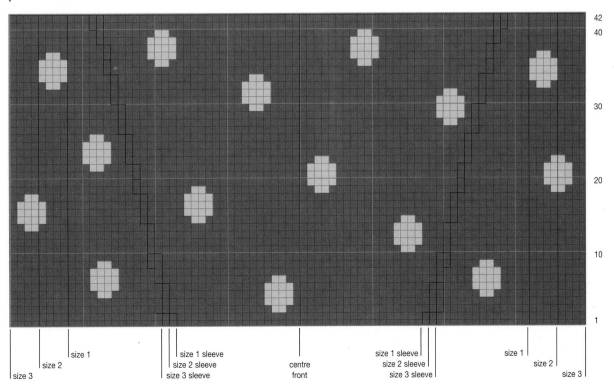

size 3
size 2
size 1
size 1 sleeve
size 2 sleeve
size 3 sleeve
centre front
size 1 sleeve
size 2 sleeve
size 3 sleeve
size 1
size 2
size 3

little blossom cardigan

This cardigan is guaranteed to catch everyone's eye with its scattered flowers. Its classic design means that it can be worn every day or dressed up for special occasions.

materials

4(4:5:6) 50g/1¾oz balls of Jaeger *Aqua* in main colour **M** (hot pink/India 322), 2(2:3:3) balls in **A** (off-white/Creme 301) and one ball in **B** (pastel pink/Anemone 327)

Pair each of 3¼mm(US 3) and 3¾mm(US 5) knitting needles

5(5:6:6) buttons

sizes

to fit

6–12 mths	1–2	2–3	3–4	yrs

actual measurements

chest

56	61	66	71	cm
22	24	26	28	in

length

30	33	36	38	cm
11¾	13	14	15	in

sleeve seam

18	21	23	27	cm
7	8¼	9	10½	in

tension/gauge

22 sts and 30 rows to 10cm/4in over st-st using 3¾mm(US 5) needles

abbreviations

beg beginning; **cm** centimetre(s); **cont** continu(e)(ing); **dec** decrease; **foll** follow(s)(ing); **in** inch(es); **inc** increase; **k** knit; **p** purl; **patt** pattern; **rem** remaining; **rep** repeat; **RS** right side; **st(s)** stitch(es); **st-st** stocking/stockinette stitch; **tog** together; **WS** wrong side; **yrn (yarn round needle)** bring yarn to front between needles, then wrap yarn around right needle from front to back and bring it to front again between needles to make a st

note

When working from chart, work in st-st and use separate length of yarn for each motif, twisting yarns at colour change to avoid holes.

back

With 3¼mm(US 3) needles and M, cast on
61(67:73:79) sts.
Moss/seed st row K1, [p1, k1] to end.
Rep last row 4 times more.
Change to 3¾mm(US 5) needles.
Next row (RS) Moss/seed st 5, k51(57:63:69) from
chart, moss/seed st 5.
Next row (WS) Moss/seed st 5, p51(57:63:69) from
chart, moss/seed st 5.
These last 2 rows set the position of the st-st with
moss/seed st side-slit sts.
Rep last 2 rows 3(3:5:5) times more.
Now work from chart in st-st only until chart row
50(56:62:68) has been worked, so ending with a WS
row.
shape armholes
Cont from chart, cast/bind off 5(5:6:6) sts at beg of
next 2 rows.
Cont straight on rem 51(57:61:67) sts until chart row
84(92:100:108) has been worked, so ending with a WS
row.
shape shoulders
Cast/bind off 15(17:19:21) sts at beg of next 2 rows.
Leave rem 21(23:23:25) sts on a holder.

pocket linings (make 2)

With 3¾mm(US 5) needles and M, cast on
17(19:19:21) sts.
Beg with a RS (k) row, work 20(20:22:22) rows in
st-st.
Leave sts on a holder.

left front

With 3¼mm(US 3) needles and M, cast on
34(37:40:43) sts.
Work 5 rows in moss/seed st as for Back.
Change to 3¾mm(US 5) needles and work in st-st
from chart between lines for correct size and garment
piece, keeping 5 sts in moss/seed st in M at beg and
end of first 8(8:12:12) rows and then at end of every
RS row and beg of every WS row for button band.
Work until 24(24:26:26) chart rows have been
worked, so ending with a WS row.
place pocket
Next row (RS) K6(7:10:11) sts in patt, slip next
17(19:19:21) sts onto a holder, k in patt across
17(19:19:21) sts of first pocket lining, k6 in patt,
moss/seed st 5 in M.
Cont to work in patt until chart row 50(56:62:68) has
been worked, so ending with a WS row.
shape armhole
Cont in patt, cast/bind off 5(5:6:6) sts at beg of next
row.
Cont straight on rem 29(32:34:37) sts until chart row
68(76:84:92) has been worked, so ending with a WS
row.
shape neck
Next row (RS) Patt to last 5 sts and slip these rem 5
moss/seed sts at front edge onto a safety pin for
neckband.
Cast/bind off 3 sts at beg of next row.
Dec 1 st at neck edge on foll 6(7:7:8) rows.
Cont straight in patt until chart row 84(92:100:108)
has been worked.
Cast/bind off rem 15(17:19:21) sts for shoulder.
Mark the position for 5(5:6:6) buttons on the button
band, the first on the 5th row of lower moss/seed st
band, the last just below the neck edge and the rem
3(3:4:4) spaced evenly between.

front, back
and sleeve
chart

key
■ M
▨ B
□ A

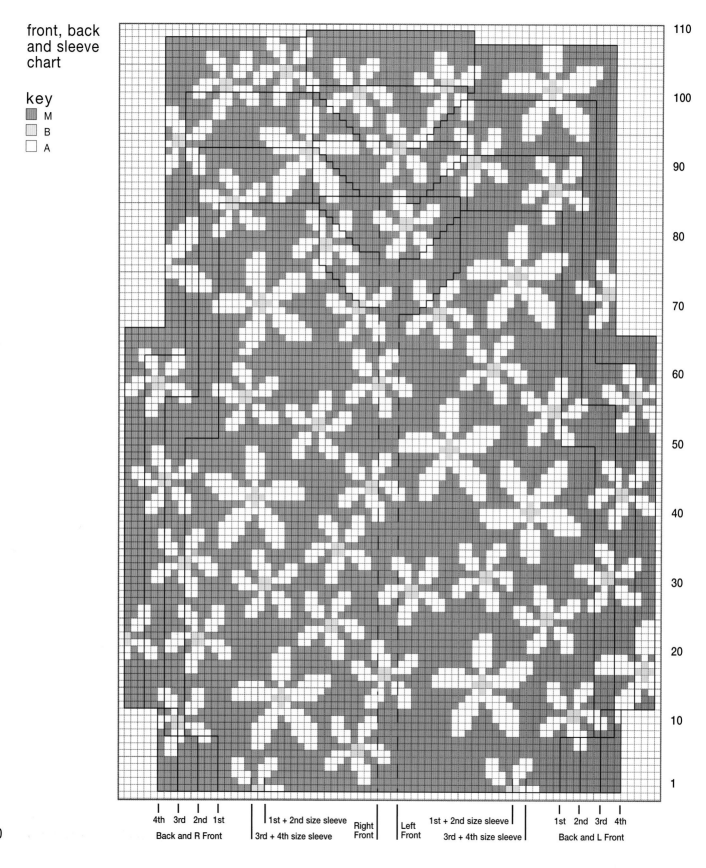

110
100
90
80
70
60
50
40
30
20
10
1

| 4th | 3rd | 2nd | 1st | | 1st + 2nd size sleeve | | Right | Left | 1st + 2nd size sleeve | | 1st | 2nd | 3rd | 4th |

Back and R Front   3rd + 4th size sleeve   Front   Front   3rd + 4th size sleeve   Back and L Front

right front

With 3¼mm(US 3) needles and M, cast on
34(37:40:43) sts.
Work 4 rows in moss/seed st as for Back.
Work first buttonhole on next row to match position
of first button as foll:
Buttonhole row (RS) K1, p2tog, yrn, p1, k1, patt
to end.
Change to 3¾mm(US 5) needles and work in st-st
from chart between lines for correct size and
garment piece, keeping 5 sts in moss/seed st in M at
beg and end of first 8(8:12:12) rows of chart and
then at beg of every RS row and end of every WS
row for buttonhole band.
Cont to work buttonholes as before to match
markers throughout, work until 24(24:26:26) chart
rows have been worked, so ending with a WS row.
place pocket
Next row (RS) Moss/seed st 5 in M, k6 in patt,
slip next 17(19:19:21) sts onto a holder, k in patt
across 17(19:19:21) sts of second pocket lining, patt
to end.
Cont to work in patt until chart row 51(57:63:69)
has been worked, so ending with a RS row.
shape armhole
Cont in patt, cast/bind off 5(5:6:6) sts at beg of next
row.
Cont straight on rem 29(32:34:37) sts until chart
row 69(77:85:93) has been worked, so ending with a
RS row.
shape neck
Next row (WS) Patt to last 5 sts and slip these rem
5 moss/seed sts at front edge onto a safety pin for
neckband.
Cast/bind off 3 sts at beg of next row.
Dec 1 st at neck edge on foll 6(7:7:8) rows.
Cont straight in patt until chart row 85(93:101:109)
has been worked.
Cast/bind off rem 15(17:19:21) sts for shoulder.

sleeves

With 3¼mm(US 3) needles and M, cast on
37(37:41:41) sts and work 5 rows in moss/seed st as
for Back. Change to 3¾mm(US 5) needles.
Beg with a RS (k) row and working in st-st from

chart, inc 1 st at each end of 5th and every foll 6th
row until there are 51(53:55:57) sts, taking all inc
sts into patt.
Cont straight until sleeve measures
18(21:23:27)cm/7(8¼:9:10½)in from cast-on edge.
Mark each end of last row, then work 6(6:7:7) rows
more.
Cast/bind off in patt.

collar

Join shoulder seams.
With WS facing, 3¼mm(US 3) needles and M,
moss/seed st 5 sts from safety pin of right front,
turn and cast/bind off 3 sts, moss/seed st rem st on
left needle, pick up and k 17 sts up Right Front
neck, k across 21(23:23:25) sts at back neck, pick up
and k 17 sts down Left Front neck and moss/seed st
5 from safety pin.
Next row Cast/bind off 3 sts, moss/seed st to end.
59(61:61:63) sts.
Work 2cm/¾in in moss/seed st.
Change to 3¾mm(US 5) needles and work 5cm/2in
more in moss/seed st.
Cast/bind off in moss/seed st.

pocket top

With RS facing, 3¼mm(US 3) needles and M, k
across 17(19:19:21) sts of pocket holder.
Work 4 rows in moss/seed st.
Cast/bind off.

to finish

Sew sleeves into armholes, joining row ends above
markers to cast-/bound-off sts at underarm. Join
sleeve seams. Join side seams above moss/seed st
side slits. Sew pocket lining and pocket top edges in
place. Sew on buttons.

fair isle cardigan

The subtle colours in this design create a modern twist on the classic Fair Isle cardigan. The little collar and mother-of-pearl buttons give it a simple, uncluttered finish.

materials

1(2:2:2) 50g/1¾oz balls of Rowan *Cotton Glacé* in main colour **M** (purple/Hyacinth 787), 1(1:2:2) balls in **A** (rose pink/Bubbles 724) and one ball each in **B** (lilac/ Tickle 811), **C** (light pink/ Candy Floss 747), **D** (light green/ Bud 800), **E** (turquoise/Pier 809) and **F** (off-white/Ecru 725)

Pair each of 3mm(US 2) and 3¼mm(US 3) knitting needles

5(5:6:6) buttons

sizes

to fit

6–12 mths	1–2	2–3	3–4	yrs
actual measurements				
chest				
56	61	66	71	cm
22	24	26	28	in
length				
30	33	36	38	cm
11¾	13	14	15	in
sleeve seam				
18	21	23	27	cm
7	8¼	9	10½	in

tension/gauge

26 sts and 31 rows to 10cm/4in over patterned st-st using 3¼mm (US 3) needles

abbreviations

alt alternate; **beg** beginning; **cm** centimetre(s); **cont** continu(e)(ing); **dec** decrease; **foll** follow(s)(ing); **in** inch(es); **inc** increas(e)(ing); **k** knit; **p** purl; **patt** pattern; **rem** remaining; **rep** repeat; **RS** right side; **st(s)** stitch(es); **st-st** stocking/stockinette stitch; **tbl** through back of loop(s); **tog** together; **WS** wrong side

note

When working from chart, strand yarn not in use across WS of work, weaving into back of sts where stranded yarn crosses more than 5 sts.

back

With 3mm(US 2) needles and M, cast on
73(79:85:93) sts.
Moss/seed st row K1, [p1, k1] to end.
Rep last row 5 times more.
Change to 3¼mm(US 3) needles.
Beg with a RS (k) row, work in st-st from chart, placing
marked st centrally.
Cont straight until back measures
19(21:23:24)cm/7½(8¼:9:9½)in from cast-on edge,
ending with a WS row.
shape armholes
Cont from chart, cast/bind off 5(5:6:6) sts at beg of
next 2 rows.
Cont straight on rem 63(69:73:81) sts until back
measures 30(33:36:38)cm/11¾(13:14:15)in from cast-
on edge, ending with a WS row.
shape shoulders
Cast/bind off 19(21:22:25) sts at beg of next 2 rows.
Leave rem 25(27:29:31) sts on a holder.

pocket lining (make 1)

With 3¼mm(US 3) needles and B (lilac), cast on
19(21:23:25) sts.
Beg with a RS (k) row, work 20(20:22:22) rows in st-st.
Leave sts on a holder.

left front

With 3mm(US 2) needles and M, cast on 39(41:45:49) sts.
Work 6 rows in moss/seed st as for Back, but inc 1 st at
end of last row for 2nd size only. 39(42:45:49) sts.
Change to 3¼mm(US 3) needles and work in st-st from
chart beg with same st as Back (3rd st to left of centre
marked st for Right Front), keeping 5 sts in moss/seed st
at end of every RS row and beg of every WS row for
button band. Work until 22(22:24:24) chart rows have
been worked, so ending with a WS row.
place pocket
Next row (RS) K9(10:11:13) sts in patt, slip next
19(21:23:25) sts onto a holder, k in patt across
19(21:23:25) sts of pocket lining, k6 in patt, moss/seed
st 5 in M.
Cont to work in patt until front measures
19(21:23:24)cm/7½(8¼:9:9½)in from cast-on edge,
ending with a WS row (RS row for right front).
shape armhole
Cont in patt, cast/bind off 5(5:6:6) sts at beg of next
row.
Cont straight on rem 34(37:39:43) sts until front
measures 25(28:30:32)cm/10(11:11¾:12½)in from cast-
on edge, ending with a RS row (WS row for right front).
shape neck
Cast/bind off 3 sts at beg of next row.
Next row Patt to last 2 sts and slip these last 2 sts at
front edge onto a safety pin for collar.
Keeping chart patt correct, cast/bind off 3 sts at beg
(neck edge) of next and foll alt row, then dec 1 st at neck
edge on foll 4(5:6:7) alt rows.
Cont until front matches Back to shoulder.
shape shoulder
Cast/bind off rem 19(21:22:25) sts.
Mark the position for 5(5:6:6) buttons on the button
band, the first on the 5th row of lower moss/seed st
band, the last just below the neck edge with the rem
3(3:4:4) spaced evenly between.

right front

Work as for Left Front, but omitting pocket, working 5
moss/seed sts for buttonhole band at beg of RS rows and
end of WS rows and noting bracketed exceptions (so
reversing all shaping) **and at the same time** work
buttonholes to match markers on Left Front when

reached as foll:
1st buttonhole row (RS) K1, p2tog, make 2 *yarn overs* by wrapping yarn around right-hand needle from front to back and to front again and then over right-hand needle again ready to work next st, k2tog, patt to end.
2nd buttonhole row (WS) Work in patt, working [p1, k1tbl] into double yarn over of previous row.

sleeves

With 3mm(US 2) needles and M, cast on 35(37:39:41) sts and work 6 rows in moss/seed st as for Back.
Change to 3¼mm(US 3) needles.
Beg with a RS (k) row and working in st-st from chart, inc 1 st at each end of 5th and every foll 4th row until there are 57(63:67:73) sts, taking all inc sts into patt.
Cont straight until sleeve measures 18(21:23:27)cm/7(8¼:9:10½)in from cast-on edge.
Mark each end of last row, then work 6(6:7:7) rows more.
Cast/bind off in patt.

collar

Join shoulder seams.
With WS facing, 3mm(US 2) needles and M, moss/seed st 2 sts from safety pin on Right Front, turn and moss/seed st 2, pick up and k 13(13:15:15) sts up right front neck, k across 25(27:29:31) sts at back neck, pick up and k 13(13:15:15) sts down left front neck and moss/seed st 2 from safety pin. 55(57:63:65) sts.
Work 2cm/¾in in moss/seed st.
Change to 3¼mm(US 3) needles and work a further 4cm/1½in in moss/seed st.
Cast/bind off.

pocket top

With RS facing, 3mm(US 2) needles and M, k across 19(21:23:25) sts of pocket holder.
Work 4 rows in moss/seed st.
Cast/bind off.

to finish

Sew sleeves into armholes, joining row ends above markers to cast-/bound-off sts at underarm. Join side and sleeve seams. Sew pocket lining and pocket top edges in place. Sew on buttons.

fair isle chart

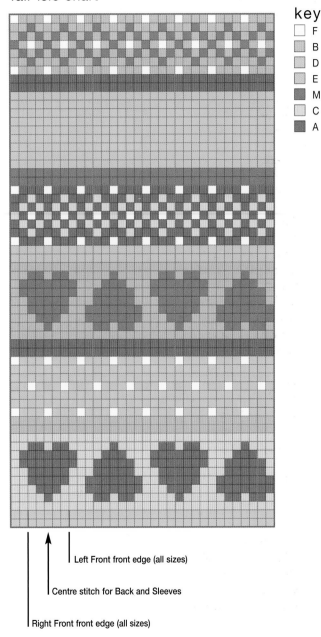

key
☐ F
▨ B
▨ D
▨ E
▨ M
☐ C
▨ A

Left Front front edge (all sizes)

Centre stitch for Back and Sleeves

Right Front front edge (all sizes)

dots & stripes blanket

A blanket is the perfect gift for a newborn baby. Ideal for boys or girls and in lightweight yarn, it will become a much-loved heirloom and be cherished for years.

materials

4 50g/1¾oz balls of Rowan *4 ply Soft* in main colour **M** (lilac/Buzz 375), 2 balls each in **A** (lime green/Goblin 379) and **B** (turquoise/Splash 373) and one ball in **C** (white/Nippy 376)
Pair of long 3¼mm(US 3) knitting needles

size

Approximately 62cm/24⅓in by 87cm/34¼in.

tension/gauge

28 sts and 36 rows to 10cm/4in over st-st using 3¼mm(US 3) needles

abbreviations

beg beginning; **cm** centimetre(s); **in** inch(es); **k** knit; **p** purl; **RS** right side; **st(s)** stitch(es); **st-st** stocking/stockinette stitch

note

The squares are all worked in st-st beg with a RS (k) row and have 7 moss/seed sts in M between each square and 3cm/1¼in in moss/seed st between each line of squares. Spot squares are worked from two charts (small spots and large spots) and in nine colour combinations. Use separate small balls of yarn for each spot square, twisting yarns at colour change to avoid holes.

squares patterns

striped squares
Worked over 25 sts and 32 rows.
Stripe square 1 – 2 rows C, 4 rows B, 3 rows A, 4 rows C, 5 rows M, 3 rows B, 4 rows C, 4 rows A, 3 rows B.
Stripe square 2 – 4 rows A, 6 rows B, 2 rows C, 5 rows M, 3 rows A, 4 rows C, 4 rows M, 4 rows B.

large and small spot squares
Worked over 25 sts and 32 rows.
Spot square 1 – Background in C with spots in M.
Spot square 2 – Background in A with spots in M.
Spot square 3 – Background in B with spots in C.
Spot square 4 – Background in B with spots in M.
Spot square 5 – Background in A with spots in B.
Spot square 6 – Background in A with spots in C.
Spot square 7 – Background in C with spots in B.
Spot square 8 – Background in C with spots in A.
Spot square 9 – Background in B with spots in A.

to make
With 3¼mm(US 3) needles and M, cast on 175 sts.
Moss/seed st row K1, [p1, k1] to end.
This last row forms moss/seed st and is repeated.
Work 4cm/1½in in moss/seed st, ending with a WS row.
first line of squares
Next row (RS) K1, [p1, k1] 5 times, k 25 sts of first row of *large spot square 1*, k1M, [p1M, k1M] 3 times, k25 sts of first row of *stripe square 1*, moss/seed st 7 in M, k first row of *large spot square 2*, moss/seed st 7M, k first row *stripe square 1*, moss/seed st 7M, k first row of *large spot square 3*, moss/seed st 11M.
This last row sets the position of the first line of large spot and stripe 1 squares with 7 moss/seed sts in M between squares and 11-st moss/seed st borders in M at each edge.
When all 32 rows of first line of squares have been worked, work 3cm/1¼in in moss/seed st in M, ending with a WS row. (**Note** Always end horizontal bands of moss/seed st with a WS row, so RS will be facing for starting next line of squares.)
Cont to work moss/seed st borders in M, work 6 more lines of squares with 3cm/1¼in of moss/seed st in M

between them, working squares in each line as foll:
2nd line of squares
Stripe square 2, small spot square 4, stripe square 2, small spot square 1, stripe square 2.
3rd line of squares
Large spot square 5, stripe square 1, large spot square 3, stripe square 1, large spot square 2.
4th line of squares
Stripe square 2, small spot square 6, stripe square 2, small spot square 7, stripe square 2.
5th line of squares
Large spot square 4, stripe square 1, large spot square 8, stripe square 1, large spot square 9.
6th line of squares
Stripe square 2, small spot square 3, stripe square 2, small spot square 6, stripe square 2.
7th line of squares
Large spot square 2, stripe square 1, large spot square 9, stripe square 1, large spot square 1.
When 7th line of squares has been worked, work 4cm/1½in in moss/seed st in M.
Cast/bind off in moss/seed st.

small spot chart   **large spot chart**

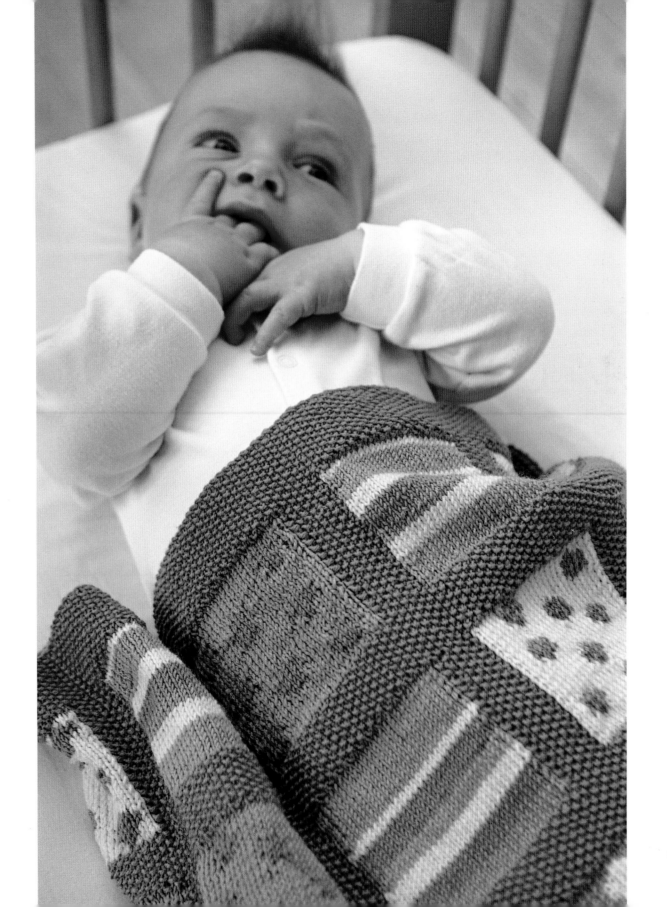

wrap up warm

ship ahoy! sweater

This nautical knitted sweater, with boat and fishes, looks jolly and is lovely and comfortable too.

materials

3(4:4:5) 50g/1¾oz balls of Rowan *Cotton Glacé* in main colour **M** (blue/Splendour 810) and one ball each in **A** (red/Poppy 741) and **B** (yellow/Sunny 802)

One 50g/1¾oz ball each of Jaeger *Aqua* in **C** (navy blue/Deep 320) and **D** (light green/Herb 303)

Pair of 3¼mm(US 3) knitting needles

sizes

to fit

6–12 mths	1–2	2–3	3–4	yrs

actual measurements

chest

56	61	66	71	cm
22	24	26	28	in

length

30	33	36	38	cm
11¼	13	14	15	in

sleeve seam

18	21	23	27	cm
7	8¼	9	10¾	in

tension/gauge

23 sts and 32 rows to 10cm/4in over st-st using 3¼mm(US 3) needles

abbreviations

alt alternate; **beg** beginning; **cm** centimetre(s); **cont** continu(e)(ing); **dec** decrease; **foll** follow(s)(ing); **in** inch(es); **inc** increase; **k** knit; **p** purl; **patt** pattern; **rem** remaining; **rep** repeat; **RS** right side; **st(s)** stitch(es); **st-st** stocking/stockinette stitch; **tog** together; **WS** wrong side

note

When working from charts, use separate small balls of yarn for each motif, twisting yarns at colour change to avoid holes.

back

With 3¼mm(US 3) needles and C, cast on
64(70:76:82) sts.
Beg with a RS (k) row, work 6 rows in st-st.
Change to M.
1st rib row (RS) K3(2:3:2), [p2, k2] to last 1(0:1:0)
st, k1(0:1:0).
2nd rib row P3(2:3:2), [k2, p2] to last 1(0:1:0) st,
p1(0:1:0).
Rep last 2 rows 3 times more.**
Beg with a RS (k) row, work 48(54:60:64) rows in
st-st.
shape armholes
Cont in st-st, cast/bind off 5 sts at beg of next 2 rows.
54(60:66:72) sts.
Cont straight for 36(38:42:46) rows more.
shape shoulders
Cast/bind off 12(14:16:18) sts at beg of next 2 rows.
Leave rem 30(32:34:36) sts on a holder.

front

Work as for Back to **.
Beg with a RS (k) row, work 6(10:10:12) rows in st-st,
so ending with a WS (p) row.
place fish chart
Next row (RS) K13(16:18:21)M, k across 14 sts of
first row of fish chart, k to end in M.
Cont in st-st foll chart until all 7 chart rows have been
worked.
Cont in st-st in M only for 25(25:39:39) rows more,
so ending with a WS row.
place boat chart
Next row (RS) K20(23:26:29)M, k across 25 sts of
first row of boat chart, k to end in M.
Cont in st-st foll chart until chart row 10(12:4:6) has
been worked.
shape armholes
Keeping chart correct, cast/bind off 5 sts at beg of
next 2 rows, then cont straight on rem 54(60:66:72)
sts until all 29 chart rows have been worked.
Cont in st-st in M only for 3(7:3:9) rows more, so
ending with a WS row.
shape neck
Next row (RS) K21(24:27:30), turn and cont on
these sts only, leaving rem sts on a spare needle.

Cast/bind off 3 sts at beg (neck edge) of next row, 2
sts at beg of foll 1(1:2:3) alt rows and dec 1 st at beg
of next 4(5:4:3) alt rows. 12(14:16:18) sts.
Work 4(2:2:2) rows.
Cast/bind off for shoulder.
With RS facing, slip 12 sts at centre front onto a
holder, rejoin yarn to rem sts and complete to match
first side.

left sleeve

With 3¼mm(US 3) needles and C, cast on
28(30:32:34) sts.
Beg with a RS (k) row, work 6 rows in st-st.
Change to M.
1st rib row (RS) K3(2:3:2), [p2, k2] to last 1(0:1:0)
st, k1(0:1:0).
2nd rib row P3(2:3:2), [k2, p2] to last 1(0:1:0) st,
p1(0:1:0).
Rep last 2 rows 3 times more.
Beg with a RS (k) row and working in st-st, inc 1 st at
each end of 3rd(7th:1st:5th) row and foll 2(1:2:1)
3rd(3rd:4th:4th) rows. 34(34:38:38) sts.
Work 1(0:1:1) row, so ending with a WS row.
place fish chart
Next row (RS) K12(12:14:14)M, k across 14 sts of
first row of fish chart, k8(8:10:10)M.
Cont in st-st foll chart until all 7 chart rows have been
worked and **at the same time** cont to inc as set on
next(2nd:2nd:2nd) row and then on every foll
3rd(3rd:4th:4th) row until there are 56(60:64:68) sts.
Cont straight until sleeve measures
18(21:23:27)cm/7(8¼:9:10¾)in from beg of rib.
Mark each end of last row, then work 6 rows more.
Cast/bind off.

right sleeve
Work as for Left Sleeve, but omitting fish.

neckband
Join right shoulder seam.
With RS facing, 3¼mm(US 3) needles and M, pick up
and k 19(19:21:21) sts down left front neck, k across
10 sts at centre front, pick up and k 19(19:21:21) sts

up right front neck, then k across 30(32:34:36) sts
at back neck and inc 2 sts evenly. 80(82:88:90) sts.
Beg with a 2nd rib row, work 3cm/1¼in in rib as
for Back, ending with a 2nd rib row.
Change to C and beg with a RS (k) row, work 6
rows in st-st.
Cast/bind off.

to finish

Join left shoulder and neckband seam. Sew sleeves
into armholes, joining row ends above markers to
cast-/bound-off sts at underarm. Join side and
sleeve seams.

fish motif

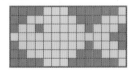

boat motif

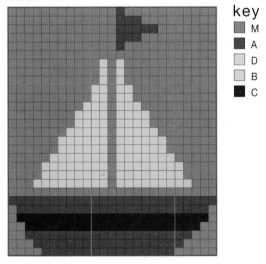

key

key
M
A
D
B
C

kitten & puppy sweaters

In gentle pastel colourways, these knits look sweet on babies. The soft yarn will keep them warm and cosy on cool days.

materials

Kitten: 2(2:3) 50g/1¾oz balls of Jaeger *Baby Merino* 4 ply in main colour **M** (ivory/Pearl 103) and 1 50g/1¾oz of Jaeger *Matchmaker* 4 ply in **A** (pale pink/Princess 126) and **B** (dark pink/Red Check 094)

Puppy: 2(2:3) 50g/1¾oz balls of Jaeger *Baby Merino* 4 ply in main colour **M** (white/White 102) and 1 50g/1¾oz ball in **A** (pale green/Mint 101) and **B** (green/Spearmint 118)

Pair each of 2¾mm(US 2) and 3¼mm(US 3) knitting needles

3 buttons

sizes

to fit

3–6	6–9	9–12	mths

actual measurements

chest

51	55	61	cm
20	21¼	24	in

length to shoulder

25	28	30	cm
9¾	11	12	in

sleeve

15	17	19	cm
6	6¾	7½	in

tension/gauge

28 sts and 36 rows to 10cm/4in over st-st using 3¼mm(US 3) needles

abbreviations

alt alternate; **cm** centimetre(s); **cont** continue; **dec** decreas(e)(ing); **inc** increas(e)(ing); **in** inch(es); **k** knit; **k2tog** knit next 2 sts together; **mm** millimetre(s); **p** purl; **p2tog** purl next 2 sts together; **PM** place marker; **rem** remain(ing); **RS** right side; **st(s)** stitch(es); **st-st** stocking/stockinette stitch; **yo (yarn over needle)** take yarn over right needle to make a st; **yrn (yarn round needle)** wrap yarn around right needle from front to back and to front again between needles to make a st; **WS** wrong side

note

When working from chart, use separate small balls of yarn for each colour area and twist yarns at colour change to avoid holes.

back

**With 2¾mm(US 2) needles and M, cast on 73(79:87) sts.

1st row (moss/seed st) K1, *p1, k1, rep from * to end.

Rep this row 6 times more.

Change to 3¼mm(US 3) needles and B.

1st row (WS) P.

2nd row K.

3rd row Change to M and p 1 row.

Now work lace panel as folls:

1st row (RS) K4(7:11), *yo, k2tog, k14: rep from * ending last rep k3(6:10).

2nd, 4th, 6th and 8th rows (WS) P.

3rd row K2(5:9), *yo, k2tog, k2, yo, k2tog, k10: rep from * ending last rep k1(4:8).

5th row K8(3:7), *yo, k2tog, k6: rep from * ending last rep k7(2:6).

7th row K10(1:1), yo, k2tog, [k2, yo, k2tog] 1(0:1) time, *k10, yo, k2tog, k2, yo, k2tog; rep from * to last 9(12:0) sts, k9(10:0), [yo, k2tog] 0(1:0) time.

9th row K12(15:3), *yo, k2tog, k14; rep from * ending last rep k11(14:2).

Change to A and work 2 rows.

Change to M.**

Beg with a p (WS) row, cont in M only and work 33(39:43) rows st-st, so ending with a p row.

shape armholes

Cast/bind off 4(5:6) sts at beg of next 2 rows. 65(69:75) sts.

Cont straight for 34(38:42) more rows, ending with a p row.

shape shoulders

Next row Cast/bind off 18(20:22) sts, k to end.

Next row K18(20:22) sts, turn, leaving rem 29(29:31) sts on a holder for back neck.

Knit 2 rows for button shoulder band.

Cast/bind off knitwise.

front

Work as given for Back from ** to **.

Beg with a p (WS) row, cont in M only and work 25(33:39) rows st-st.

Chart placement row (RS) K22(25:28), k across 29 sts of 1st row of chart, k22(25:29).

This row sets the position of the chart. Work 7(5:3) rows more in st-st, while keeping chart correct.

shape armholes

Keeping chart correct, cast/bind off 4(5:6) sts at beg of next 2 rows. 65(69:75) sts.

Cont in st-st until all 24 chart rows have been worked, then cont in M only and work 8(10:10) rows st-st, so ending with a p row.

shape neck

1st row (RS) K26 (28:30), turn and cont on these sts only, leaving rem sts on a spare needle.

2nd row Cast/bind off 3 sts (neck edge), p to end. 23(25:27) sts.

3rd–5th rows Work in st-st dec 1 st at neck edge. 20(22:24) sts.

6th–9th rows Work in st-st dec 1 st at neck edge on 7th and 9th rows. 18(20:22) sts.

3rd size only

Work 2 rows st-st.

all sizes

Next row K.

Work 6(6:4) rows.

Next row (make buttonholes) (RS) K5, yo, k2tog, k5(6:7), yo, k2tog, k4(5:6).

K 2 rows.

Cast/bind off knitwise.

With RS facing, slip 13(13:15) sts at centre front onto a holder, rejoin yarn to rem 26(28:30) sts, k to end.

2nd row P.

3rd row Cast/bind off 3 sts (neck edge), k to end.

4th–6th rows Work in st-st dec 1 st at neck edge. 20(22:24) sts.

7th–10th rows Work in st-st dec 1 st at neck edge on 7th and 9th rows. 18(20:22) sts.

3rd size only

Work 2(2:4) rows st-st.

Cast/bind off.

sleeves

With 2¾mm(US 2) needles and M, cast on 35(39:43) sts.

Work 7 rows in moss/seed st as given for Back.
Change to 3¼mm(US 3) needles and B.

1st row (WS) P.

2nd row K.

3rd row Change to M and p, inc 1 st at each end on 2nd and 3rd sizes only. 35 (41:45) sts.

Now work lace panel as follows:

1st row (RS) K1, (4:6), [yo, k2tog, k14] twice, yo, k2tog, k0(3:5).

2nd, 4th, 6th and 8th rows (WS) P.

3rd row K3(6:8), [yo, k2tog, k10, yo, k2tog, k2] twice, k0(3:5).

5th row Inc in 1st st, k4(7:9), [yo, k2tog, k6] 3 times, yo, k2tog, k3(6:8), inc in last st.

7th row K8(11:13), yo, k2tog, k2, yo, k2tog, k10, yo, k2tog, k2, yo, k2tog, k7(10:12).

9th row Inc in 1st st, k9(12:14), yo, k2tog, k14, yo, k2tog, k8(11:13), inc in last st.

Beg with a WS row, cont in st-st working stripes of 2 rows A and 10 rows M **while at the same time**, inc 1 st at each end of every foll 4th row until there are 55(59:63) sts.

Cont straight until sleeve measures 15(17:19)cm/ 6(6¾:7½)in from cast-on edge.

PM at each end of last row, then work a further 5(6:7) rows.

Cast/bind off.

moss/seed stitch neckband (puppy)

**Join right shoulder seam. With RS facing, 2¾mm(US 2) needle and M, pick up and k14(14:16) sts down buttonhole band and left front neck, k across 13(13:15) sts at centre front, pick up and k14(14:16) sts up right front neck, k across 29(29:31) sts at centre back, then pick up and k4 sts up button band edge. 74(74:82) sts.*

1st row *K1, p1, rep from * to end.

2nd row P1, k1, p1, yrn, p2tog, *k1, p1 rep from * to end.

Work 2 more rows in moss/seed st.**

Cast/bind off in moss/seed st.

picot neck edging (kitten)

Work as moss/seed st neckband from ** to **, then work picot cast/bind off edge as follows:

Cast/bind-off row (WS) Cast/bind off 3(3:5) sts, *slip st from right needle back onto left needle, cast on 2 sts, cast/bind off 5 sts, rep from * to end.

to finish

Work lace edgings (optional) before making up. With centre of cast/bind-off edge of sleeve to shoulder, sew sleeves into armholes with row ends above markers, sewn to cast/bind-off sts at underarm. Join side seams. Join sleeve seams unless working optional lace edge. Sew on buttons to match buttonholes.

optional lace sleeve edging (kitten)

With RS facing, 2¾mm(US 2) needle and M, pick up and k 35(39:43) sts along sleeve edge.

picot cast/bind-off edge

Cast/bind-off row (WS) Cast/bind off 5(3:4) sts, * slip st from right needle back onto left needle, cast on 2 sts, cast/bind off 5 sts, rep from * to end. Join sleeve seam.

optional lace lower edging (kitten)

With RS facing, 2¾mm(US 2) needle and M, pick up and k73(79:87) sts from lower edge of front.

Cast/bind-off row (WS) Cast/bind off 3 sts, *slip st from right needle back onto left needle, cast on 2 sts, cast/bind off 5 sts, rep from * to end. Repeat for back lower edge.

kitten motif

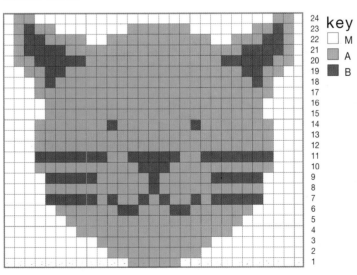

24
23
22
21
20
19
18
17
16
15
14
13
12
11
10
9
8
7
6
5
4
3
2
1

key
□ M
▨ A
▣ B

puppy motif

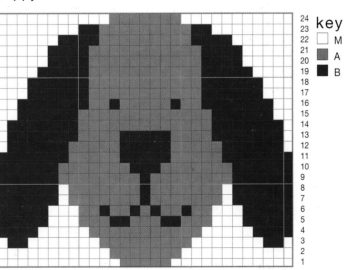

24
23
22
21
20
19
18
17
16
15
14
13
12
11
10
9
8
7
6
5
4
3
2
1

key
□ M
▨ A
■ B

outdoor snuggle

This little snuggle is great for days out with your newborn baby, and the chick motif is cute for boys or girls. It fits over clothing and can be kept on in the buggy or carrier.

materials

7 50g/1¾oz balls of *Rowan Wool Cotton* in main colour **M** (pale green/Riviera 930), 1 50g/1¾oz ball of Jaeger *Baby Merino DK* in **A** (orange/Orange 234) and 1 ball in **B** (yellow/Gold 225)
Pair each of 3mm(US 2–3) and 3¾mm(US 5) knitting needles
Spare knitting needle
40cm/16in zip fastener to match orange (**A**)

size

to fit

0–3 mths

tension/gauge

23 sts and 32 rows to 10cm/4in over st-st using 3mm(US 2–3) needles

abbreviations

alt alternate; **beg** begin(ning); **cm** centimetre(s); **cont** continue; **dec** decreas(e)(ing); **foll(s)** follow(s)(ing); **inc** increas(e)(ing); **in** inch(es); **k** knit; **k2tog** knit next 2 sts together; **mm** millimetre(s); **p** purl; **p2tog** purl next 2 sts together; **patt** pattern; **rem** remain(ing); **RS** right side; **st(s)** stitch(es); **st-st** stocking/stockinette stitch

note

When working from chart, use separate small balls of yarn for each colour area and twist yarns at colour change to avoid holes.

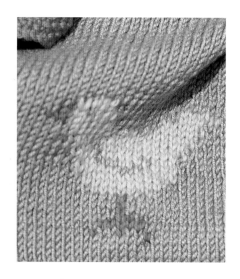

149th row Dec, k to end. 66 sts.
150th row Cast/bind off 5 sts, p to end. 61 sts.
151st row Cast/bind off 3 sts, k to end. 58 sts.
152nd row Cast/bind off 4 sts, p to end. 54 sts.
153rd–156th row Cast/bind off 3 sts, work to end. 42 sts.
157th row Cast/bind off 3 sts, k to last 2 sts, k2tog. 38 sts.
158th row P2tog, p to end. 37 sts.
159th row Cast/bind off 3 sts, k to last 2 sts, k2tog. 33 sts.
160th row P.
161st row Cast/bind off 7 sts, k to last 2 sts, k2tog. 25 sts.
162nd–163rd row As 160th–161st row. 17 sts.
164th row P.
165th row Cast/bind off 7 sts, k to end. 10 sts.
166th row P.
Cast/bind off.

right front

Work as given for Left Front, reversing all shaping (an easy way to do this is to foll patt for Left Front but read p for k and k for p), and ignoring motif.

back
right back
Work to ## of Right Front and leave sts on spare needle.
left back
Work to ## of Left Front and cont as folls:
back
33rd row K48 from left back, cast on 1 st, k48 from right back. 97 sts.
34th–94th rows Dec each end of 39th, 51st, 63rd, 75th, 87th rows. 87 sts.
shape arms
95th–128th rows Cast on 2 sts, work to end. 155 sts.
129th–142nd rows Work in st-st without shaping.
shape shoulders
143rd–160th rows Cast/bind off 3 sts, work to end. 101 sts.

left front

Start at foot. With 3¾mm (US 5) needles and M, cast on 11 sts.
1st row K.
2nd row Cast on 3 sts, p to end. 14 sts.
3rd row Inc in first st, k to end. 15 sts.
4th–7th rows As 2nd–3rd rows. 23 sts.
8th row Cast on 2 sts, p to end. 25 sts.
9th row K.
10th–26th rows As 8th–9th rows. 43 sts.
27th row K2tog, k to end. 42 sts.
28th–31st rows As 8th–9th rows. 46 sts.
32nd row As 8th row. 48 sts. ##
33rd–94th rows Cont in st-st, dec 1 st at beg of 39th, 51st, 63rd, 75th and 87th rows. 43 sts.
shape arm
95th–106th rows Continue in st-st and cast on 2 sts beg each k row. 55 sts.
107th row Start motif in A, cast on 2 sts, k21, work 23 sts of 1st row of chart, k11. 57 sts.
108th row P11, work 2nd row of chart, p23.
109th–117th rows Cont casting on 2 sts at beg of every k row, and working motif. 67 sts.
118th–148th rows Work on st-st without shaping, completing motif.

shape neck
161st row Cast/bind off 7 sts, k31, cast/bind off 25 sts, k to end.
162nd row Cast/bind off 7 sts, work to end. 31 sts.
163rd row Cast/bind off 5 sts, work to end. 26 sts.
164th row Cast/bind off 7 sts, work to last 2 sts, dec 18 sts.
165th row Dec, work to end. 17 sts.
166th row Cast/bind off 7 sts, work to end. 10 sts.
Rejoin yarn to rem sts at neck edge and work 163rd to 166th rows.

hand flap
left hand
With 3¾mm(US 5) needles and M, cast on 3 sts and p 1 row.
2nd–14th row Working in st-st, cast on 2 sts beg of next and every alt row. 17 sts.
15th row P.
16th row Cast on 3 sts, k to end. 20 sts.
17th–31st row Work in st-st without shaping.
32nd–40th row Cast/bind off 3 sts beg of next and every alt row. 5 sts.
41st row P.
Cast/bind off.
right hand
Work as given for Left Hand, but reversing all shaping (work k as p and p as k).

edging
RS facing, with 3mm(US 2–3) needles and A, pick up and k33 sts along straight edges of flaps.
1st row *K1, p1, rep from * to end.
2nd row As 1st row.
Cast/bind off in moss/seed stitch.

hood
With 3mm(US 2–3) needles and A, cast on 101 sts and work 6 rows in moss/seed st.
Change to 3¾mm(US 5) needles and M, work in st-st until hood measures 16cm 6¼in, ending with a p row.

shape top of hood
1st row K50, cast/bind off 1 st, k50.
2nd row On 50 sts p48, p2tog. 49 sts.
3rd row K2tog, k to end. 48 sts.
4th and alt rows P.
5th row Cast/bind off 2 sts, k to end. 46 sts.
7th row As 5th row. 44 sts.
9th row Cast/bind off 4 sts, k to end. 40 sts.
11th row Cast/bind off 4 sts, k to end. 36 sts.
12th row P.
Cast/bind off.
Rejoin yarn to rem sts and work to match, reversing all shaping.

to finish
Weave in any loose ends. With RS together, pin hand flaps to back. With RS facing, pin fronts to back (front arm will overlap hand flap). Starting at neck edge, sew around garment (shoulder, hand, underarm, side seam, 1st leg, 2nd leg and back to neck). Sew centre back seam of hood. Pin hood to neck, starting and finishing 3 sts from centre front and sew into place. Insert zip fastener then join seam between bottom of zip fastener and crotch.

chick motif

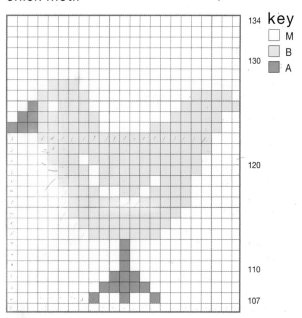

134
130
120
110
107

key
☐ M
☐ B
■ A

hearts & stars blanket

This blanket is great for family picnics or just keeping on the sofa for cold evenings. It looks great in almost any colour, so why not knit it in your own favourite?

materials

14 50g/1¾oz balls of Rowan *Handknit DK Cotton* in orange/Flame 254
Pair of extra-long 4mm(US 6) knitting needles

size

Approximately 83cm/32¾in by 110cm/43¼in

tension/gauge

20 sts and 28 rows to 10cm/4in over st-st using 4mm(US 6) needles

abbreviations

cm centimetre(s); **in** inch(es); **k** knit; **p** purl; **rep** repeat; **RS** right side; **st(s)** stitch(es); **st-st** stocking/stockinette stitch; **WS** wrong side

note

The blanket can also be worked back and forth in rows (not in rounds) with a long circular needle.

to make

With 4mm(US 6) needles, cast on 167 sts.
Moss/seed st row K1, [p1, k1] to end.
Rep this row 9 times more.

place charts

***Next row (RS)** *K1, [p1, k1] 3 times, work
across 25 sts of first row of star chart, k1, [p1, k1] 3
times, work across 25 sts of first row of heart chart;
rep from * once more, k1, [p1, k1] 3 times, work
across 25 sts of first row of star chart, k1, [p1, k1] 3
times.

This row sets the position of the first line of charts
with 7 moss/seed sts between each chart and at
each side edge.

Work as set until all 36 chart rows have been
completed.

Work 10 moss/seed st rows as set, so ending with a
WS row.**

Next row (RS) *K1, [p1, k1] 3 times, work across 25
sts of first row of heart chart, k1, [p1, k1] 3 times,
work across 25 sts of first row of star chart; rep from *
once more, k1, [p1, k1] 3 times, work across 25 sts of
first row of heart chart, k1, [p1, k1] 3 times.

This row sets the position of the second line of charts
with 7 moss/seed sts between each chart and at
each side edge.

Work as set until all 36 chart rows have been
completed.

Work 10 moss/seed st rows as set, so ending with a
WS row.***

Rep the 92 rows from *** to *** twice more and then
rep the 46 rows from *** to ** once more.

Cast/bind off in moss/seed st.

key
K on RS rows and P on WS rows
P on RS rows and K on WS rows

star chart

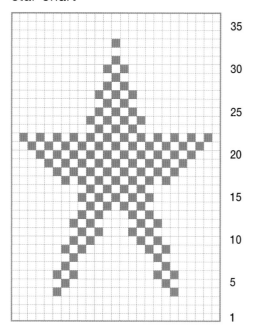

heart chart

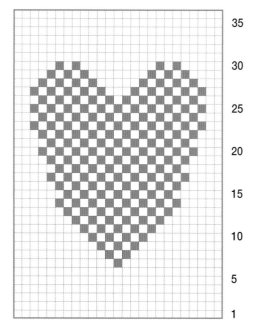

a boy's own jacket

A great jacket for winter days. The snuggly yarn will keep the chill out and keep your little one warm and toasty even in the coldest weather.

materials

3(3:3) 50g/1¾oz balls of Rowan *Calmer* in each of **A** (pale blue/ Calmer 463) and **B** (dark blue/ Slosh 479)
Pair of 5mm(US 8) knitting needles
Stitch holders
30(30:35)cm/12(12:14)in chunky open-ended zip fastener

sizes

to fit

6–12mths	1–2	2–3	yrs

actual measurements

chest

58	63	68	cm
23	24¾	26¾	in

length to shoulder

30	33	36	cm
11¾	13	14¼	in

sleeve seam

18	21	23	cm
7	8¼	9	in

tension/gauge

21 sts and 30 rows to 10cm/4in over st-st using 5mm(US 8) needles

abbreviations

alt alternate; **beg** begin(ning); **cm** centimetre(s); **cont** continue; **dec** decreas(e)(ing); **foll(s)** follow(s)(ing); **in** inch(es); **inc** increas(e)(ing); **k** knit; **k2tog** knit next 2 sts together; **k3tog** knit next 3 sts together; **m1** make one st by picking up and working into the back of the loop lying between last sts and next st; **mm** millimetre(s); **p** purl; **PM** place marker; **psso** pass slipped stitch over; **rem** remain(ing); **rep** repeat; **RS** right side; **s1** slip one stitch; **skpo** s1, k1, psso; **st(s)** stitch(es); **st-st** stocking/stockinette stitch; **WS** wrong side

back

With 5mm(US 8) needles and A, cast on 62(66:70) sts.
1st row (RS) K2, *p2, k2, rep from * to end.
2nd row (WS) P2, *k2, p2, rep from * to end.
Rep these 1st and 2nd rows for 4cm/1½in, ending with a 1st row.
Next row (WS) P.
Beg with a k (RS) row, work in st-st in 8-row stripes of B and A, until back measures 17(19:21)cm/6¾(7½:8¼)in from beg, ending with a p row.

shape armholes

Cast/bind off 5 sts at beg of next 2 rows. 52(56:60) sts.
Cont straight, keeping stripe patt correct, until back measures 30(33:36)cm/11¾(13:14¼)in from beg, ending with a p row.

shape shoulders

Cast/bind off 15(16:17) sts at beg of next 2 rows.
Leave rem 22(24:26) sts on a holder.

left front

With 5mm(US 8) needles and A, cast on 31(33:35) sts.
1st row *K2, p2, rep from * to last 3(1:3) sts, k3(1:3).
2nd row K1, p2(0:2), *k2, p2, rep from * to end.
Rep these 2 rows for 4cm/1½in, ending with a 1st row.
Next row (WS) K1, p to end.
Beg with a k (RS) row, work in st-st in 8-row stripes of B and A, working 1 st at front edge as a k st on every row.
Work straight until front measures 6(7:8)cm/2¼(2¾:3)in from beg, ending with a p row.

work pocket

Next row K10(11:12), turn and leave rem sts on first holder, cast on 18 sts, p to end.
Cont in st-st keeping striped patt correct on these 28(29:30) sts only and work a further 19 rows, so ending with a k row.
Next row Cast/bind off 18 sts, leave rem 10(11:12) sts on second holder.
With RS facing, rejoin yarn to 21(22:23) sts on first holder, k to end.
Keeping 1 st at front edge as a k st on every row, work

20 rows in striped st-st.

Next row (WS) K1, p20(21:22), p across 10(11:12) sts on second holder.

Cont straight, keeping 1 st at front edge as a k st on every row, until right front measures 17(19:21)cm/6¾(7½:8¼)in from beg, ending with a p row.

shape armhole

Cast/bind off 5 sts at beg of next row. 26(28:30) sts. Cont straight until work is 7(9:11) rows less than back at shoulder.

shape neck

1st row WS facing, cast/bind off 4 sts, p to last st, k1.

2nd row K, PM at neck edge.

3rd row Cast/bind off 4 sts, p to last st, k1.

4th and alt rows K.

5th row Cast/bind off 2 sts, work to end.

7th row Cast/bind off 1 st, work to end.

2nd size only

Rep 6th and 7th rows once.

3rd size only

Rep 6th and 7th rows twice.

all sizes

Next row Cast/bind off.

right front

With 5mm(US 8) needles and A, cast on 31(33:35) sts.

1st row (RS) K3(1:3), *p2, k2, rep from * to end.

2nd row (WS) *P2, k2, rep from * to last 3(1:3) sts, p2(0:2), k1.

Rep these 2 rows for 4cm/1½in, ending with a 1st row.

Next row (WS) P to last st, k1.

Beg with a k (RS) row, work in st-st in 8-row stripes of B and A, working 1 st at front edge as a k st on every row.

Work straight until front measures 6(7:8)cm/2¼(2¾:3)in from beg, ending with a p row.

work pocket

Next row (RS) K21(22:23), turn and leave rem 10(11:12) sts on first holder.

Beg with a p row and keeping 1 st at front edge as a k

st on every row, work 20 rows in striped st-st. Leave sts on second holder.

With RS facing, rejoin yarn to 10(11:12) sts on first holder and cast on 18 sts, k these sts then k across 10(11:12) sts on first holder. 28(29:30) sts.

Work 19 rows in striped st-st, so ending with a p row.

Next row (RS) Cast/bind off 18 sts, k to end.

Next row P10(11:12), then work across 21(22:23) sts on second holder as p20(21:22), k1. 31(33:35) sts.

Cont straight, keeping 1 st at front edge as a k st on every row, until left front measures 17(19:21)cm/6¾(7½:8¼)in from beg, ending with a k row.

shape armhole

Cast/bind off 5 sts at beg of next row.

Cont straight until work is 8(10:12) rows less than back at shoulder.

shape neck

Work to match left front starting with RS facing.

hood

Join shoulder seams.

With RS facing and with 5mm(US 8) needles and A, starting at PM pick up and k 14(16:18) sts from right front neck, k across 22(24:26) sts of back neck, pick up and k 14(16:18) sts from left front neck, ending at PM. Working in st-st, beg with a p row, and 8-row stripes as before, continue as follows. Inc on given rows **only**.

4th row K23(26:29), m1, k4, m1, k23(26:29). 52(58:764) sts.

8th(10th and 12th) row K23(26:29), m1, k6, m1, k23(26:29). 54(60:66) sts.

12th(16th and 20th) row K23(26:29), m1, k8, m1, k23(26:29). 56(62:68) sts.

16th(20th and 26th) row K23(26:29), m1, k10, m1, k23(26:29). 58(64:70) sts.

Cont inc as established on every foll 4th row to 68(74:80) sts.

Work 13 rows without shaping.

shape top

Dec on given rows **only**.

1st row K31(34:37), k2tog, k2, skpo, k31(34:37). 66(72:78) sts.

5th row K30(33:36), k2tog, k2, skpo, k30(33:36). 64(70:76 sts).

9th row K29(32:35), k2tog, k2, skpo, k29(32:35). 62(68:74) sts.

Cont to dec as established on alt rows to 54(60:66) sts.

Next row P.

Next row K23(26:29), k3tog, k2, skpo, k23(26:29). 50(56:62) sts.

Next row P.

Cast/bind off.

sleeves

With 5mm(US 8) needles and A, cast on 28(28:32) sts.

1st row (RS) K1, *p2, k2, rep from * to last 3 sts, p2, k1.

2nd row (WS) P1, *k2, p2, rep from * to last 3 sts, k2, p1.

Rep these 2 rows for 4cm/1½in, ending with a 1st row.

Next row (WS) P.

Beg with a k (RS) row, work in st-st in 4-row stripes of B and A throughout, **at the same time**, inc 1 st at each end of 3rd and every foll 3rd row until there are 54(58:64) sts.

Cont straight until sleeve measures 18(21:23)cm/7(8¼:9)in from beg, PM at each end of last row, then work 7 more rows.

Cast/bind off.

hood edging

Fold cast/bind-off edge of hood in half and join seam.

With RS facing, 5mm(US 8) needles and A, pick up 2 sts per 3 rows around edge of hood.

Work 5 rows in k2, p2 rib as given for Back.

Cast/bind off in rib.

pocket edgings

With RS facing, 5mm(US 8) needles and A, pick up and k18 along edge of each pocket.

Beg with a 2nd row, work 3 rows in k2, p2 rib as given for Back.

Cast/bind off in rib.

to finish

Sew row ends of hood edging to cast/bind-off sts at front edges. With centre of cast/bind-off edge of sleeve to shoulder, sew sleeves into armholes, with row ends above PM sewn to sts cast/bind off at underarm. Join side seams and sleeve seams. Hand-sew zip fastener to front edges. Slipstitch pocket linings in place.

fancy fair isle

Taking a modern twist on a classic design, this cardigan has mother-of-pearl buttons and looks extremely cute with the matching hat.

materials

4(4:4) 50g/1¾oz balls of Jaeger *Matchmaker Merino* 4 ply in **M** (cream/Ash 731), and 1 ball in each of (ecru/Snowdrop 102), (pale green/Thyme 715), (aqua green/Mineral 741), (pale pink/Cyclamen 694), and (dark pink/Strawberry 633)
Pair of 3¼mm(US 3) knitting needles
5 mother-of-pearl buttons

sizes

cardigan to fit

6–12 mths	1–2	2–3	yrs

actual measurements

chest

56	61	66	cm
22	24	26	in

length

30	33	36	cm
12	13	14	in

sleeve length

18	21	23	cm
7	8¼	9	in

hat to fit

6–12 mths	1–2	2–3	yrs

tension/gauge

28 sts and 36 rows to 10cm/4in over st-st using 3¼mm(US 3) needles

abbreviations

alt alternate; **beg** begin(ning); **cm** centimetre(s); **cont** continue; **foll(s)** follow(s)(ing); **in** inch(es); **inc** increas(e)(ing); **k** knit; **k2tog** knit next 2 sts together; **mm** millimetre(s); **p** purl; **patt** pattern; **PM** place marker; **rem** remain(ing); **rep** repeat; **RS** right side; **st(s)** stitch(es); **st-st** stocking/stockinette stitch; **WS** wrong side; **yo (yarn over needle)** take yarn over right needles to make a st

note

When working from chart, strand yarn not in use across WS of work, weaving in where it crosses more than 4 sts.

back

With 3¼mm(US 3) needles and M, cast on 77(85:93) sts.

1st row (RS) K1, *p1, k1, rep from * to end.
2nd row (WS) P1, *k1, p1, rep from * to end.
Rep these 2 rows for 3cm/1¼in, ending with a 2nd row.
Beg with a k (RS) row, work 4 rows in st-st.
Now work 29 rows in st-st from Fair Isle chart, working between lines for correct size.
Cont in st-st in M only until back measures 17(19:21)cm/7(7½:8¼)in from cast-on edge, ending with a p row.
shape armholes
Cast/bind off 5 sts at beg of next 2 rows. 67(75:83) sts.
Cont straight until back measures 30(33:36)cm/11¾(13:14¼)in, ending with a p row.
shape shoulders
Cast/bind off 20(22:24) sts at beg of next 2 rows.
Leave rem 27(31:35) sts on a holder.

left front

** With 3¼mm(US 3) needles and M, cast on 37(41:45) sts and work 3cm/1¼in in k1, p1 rib as given for the Back ending with a 2nd row.
Beg with a k row, work 4 rows in st-st.
Now work 29 rows in st-st from Fair Isle chart, working between lines for correct size and garment piece.
Cont in st-st in M only until left front measures 17(19:21)cm/6¾(7½:8¼)in from cast-on edge, ending with a p row.**
shape armhole
Cast/bind off 5 sts at beg of next row. 32(36:40) sts.
Cont straight until left front measures 24(27:30)cm/9½(10½:11¾)in from cast-on edge, ending with a k row.
shape neck
1st row Cast/bind off 3 sts, p to end. 29(33:37) sts.
2nd row K.
3rd row Cast/bind off 2 sts, p to end. 27(31:35) sts.
Repeat 2nd and 3rd rows 2(3:4) times. 23(25:27) sts.
Next row K.

Next row Cast/bind off 1 st, p to end. 22(24:26) sts.
Repeat the last 2 rows twice. 20(22:24) sts.
Cont without shaping until left front matches Back to shoulder, ending at side edge.
Cast/bind off.

right front

Work as given for Left Front from ** to **.
Next row K.
shape armhole
Cast/bind off 5 sts at beg of next row. 32(36:40) sts.
Cont straight until right front measures 24(27:30)cm/9½(10½:11¾)in from cast-on edge, ending with a p row.
shape neck
1st row Cast/bind off 3 sts, k to end. 29 (33:37) sts.
2nd row P.
3rd row Cast/bind off 2 sts, k to end. 27(31:35) sts.
Repeat 2nd and 3rd rows 2(3:4) times. 23(25:27) sts.
Next row P.
Next row Cast/bind off 1 st, k to end. 22(24:26) sts.
Repeat the last 2 rows twice. 20(22:24) sts.
Cont without shaping until right front matches Back to shoulder, ending at side edge.
Cast/bind off.

sleeves

With 3¼mm(US 3) needles and M, cast on 37(41:45) sts and work 3cm/1¼in in k1, p1 rib as given for the Back, ending with a 2nd row.
Beg with a k (RS) row, work 4 rows in st-st.
Now work 19 rows from sleeve chart, working between lines for correct size, **at the same time**, inc and take into patt, 1 st at each end of 3rd and every foll 3rd row until there are 67(71:77) sts.
Cont straight until sleeve measures 18(21:23)cm/7(8¼:9)in from cast-on edge, PM at each end of last row.
Work 6 more rows.
Cast/bind off.

button band

Join shoulder seams.
With RS facing, 3¼mm(US 3) needles and M, pick up and k 61(67:73) sts up left front edge.
Beg with a 2nd row, work 7 rows in k1, p1 rib as given for Back.
Cast/bind off in rib.
Mark positions for 5 buttons, the first to come 1cm/¾in above lower edge, the 5th to come in the neckband, with rem 3 spaced evenly between.

buttonhole band

With RS facing, 3¼mm(US 3) needles and M, pick up and k 61(67:73) sts up right front edge.
Beg with a 2nd row, work 3 rows in k1, p1 rib as given for Back.
Next row (buttonhole row) (RS) [K1, p1] twice, [k2tog, yo, rib14(14:16)] 3 times, k2tog, yo, rib to end.
Work 3 more rows in rib.
Cast/bind off in rib.

neckband

With RS facing, 3¼mm(US 3) needles and M, pick up and k 28 sts up buttonhole band and right neck, k across 27(31:35) sts at back neck, then pick up and k 28 sts down left front neck and button band. 83(87:91) sts.
Beg with a 2nd row, work 1 row in k1, p1 rib as given for Back.
Next row (buttonhole row) (RS) K1, p1, k2tog, yo, rib to end.
Rib 5 more rows.
Cast/bind off rib.

to finish

With centre of cast/bind off edge of sleeve to shoulder, sew sleeves into armholes with row ends above markers sewn to cast/bound-off sts at underarm. Join side sleeve seams. Sew on buttons to correspond with buttonholes.

hat

With M, cast on 117(129:141) sts.
1st row (RS) K1, *p1, k1, rep from * to end.
2nd row P1, *k1, p1, rep from * to end.
Rep these 2 rows until work measures 9cm/3½in, ending with a 2nd row.
Beg with a k row, work 4(6:8) rows in st-st.
Cont in st-st and work 20 rows from chart, between lines for correct size.
Cont in A only and work 1(3:5) rows in st-st.
shape top
1st row (RS) K6, [k2tog, k4] 18(20:22) times, k2tog, k1. 98(108:118) sts.
Work 3 rows.
5th row (RS) K5, [k2tog, k3] 18(20:22) times, k2tog, k1. 79(87:95) sts.
Work 3 rows.
9th row K4, [k2tog, k2] 18(20:22) times, k2tog, k1. 60(66:72) sts.
Work 3 rows.
13th row K3, [k2tog, k1] 18(20:22) times, k2tog, k1. 41(45:49) sts.
Work 1(3:3) rows.
Next row K2, [k2tog] 18(20:22) times, k2tog, k1. 22(24:26) sts.
Work 1(1:3) rows.
Next row K1, [k2tog] 10(11:12) times, k1. 12(13:14) sts.
Next row P.
Next row [K2tog] 6(6:7) times, k0(1:0). 6(7:7) sts.
Break yarn.

to finish

Thread yarn through rem sts, pull up and join seam, reversing seam on last 5cm/2in of rib.

sleeve and hat chart

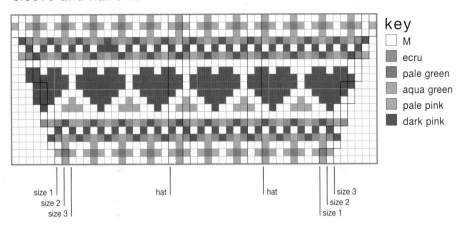

size 1
size 2
size 3
hat
hat
size 3
size 2
size 1

jacket chart

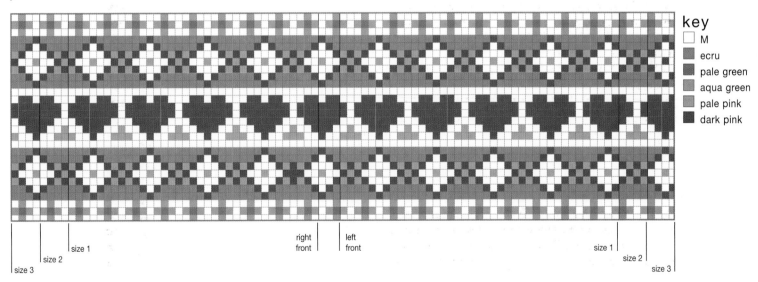

size 1
size 2
size 3
right front
left front
size 1
size 2
size 3

chunky cabled sweater

The red contrast edging makes this classic cabled sweater a little bit special. The cashmere-blend yarn is warm and cosy and shows up the cables beautifully.

materials

5(6:6:7) 50g/1¾oz balls of Debbie Bliss *Cashmerino Aran* in main colour **M** (olive/Khaki 500) and one ball in **A** (red/Red 610)
Pair each of 4½mm(US 7) and 5mm(US 8) knitting needles
Cable needle

sizes

to fit

6–12 mths	1–2	2–3	3–4	yrs

actual measurements

chest

56	61	66	71	cm
22	24	26	28	in

length

30	33	36	38	cm
11¾	13	14	15	in

sleeve seam

18	21	24	28	cm
7	8¼	9½	11	in

tension/gauge

18 sts and 30 rows to 10cm/4in over moss/seed st using 5mm(US 8) needles

abbreviations

alt alternate; **beg** beginning; **BC (back cross)** sl next 3 sts onto cable needle and hold at back, k2, sl p st from cable needle onto left needle and p1, k2 from cable needle; **C4B (cable 4 back)** sl next 2 sts onto cable needle and hold at back, k2, then k2 from cable needle; **C4F (cable 4 front)** as C4B but hold cable needle in front; **cm** centimetre(s); **cont** continu(e)(ing); **dec** decrease; **FC (front cross)** as BC but hold cable needle in front; **foll** follow(s)(ing) **in** inch(es); **inc** increase; **k** knit; **p** purl; **patt** pattern; **rem** remaining; **rep** repeat; **RS** right side; **sl** slip; **st(s)** stitch(es); **st-st** stocking/stockinette stitch; **tog** together; **Tw2L (twist 2 left)** k into back of 2nd st on left needle, k into front of first st on left needle, sl both sts off needle; **Tw2R (twist 2 right)** k into front of 2nd st on left needle, k into front of first st on left needle, sl both sts off needle; **WS** wrong side

note

Work all instructions in [ ]s the number of times stated.

back

With 4½mm(US 7) needles and A, cast on 62(67:72:82) sts.
Change to M.
1st rib row (RS) P2, [k3, p2] to end.
2nd rib row (WS) K2, [p3, k2] to end.
These last 2 rows form rib and are repeated.
Work 4cm/1½in in rib, ending with a 2nd rib row.
Inc row (RS) K and inc 4(11:10:12) sts evenly across row. 66(78:82:94) sts.
Change to 5mm(US 8) needles.
1st row (WS) K1, [p1, k1] 5(3:4:7) times, k1, p2, k1, [k1, p4, k2, p2, k1] 1(2:2:2) times, [k1, p2] 5 times, k1, [k1, p2, k2, p4, k1] 1(2:2:2) times, k1, p2, k1, [k1, p1] 5(3:4:7) times, k1.
2nd row (RS) K1, [p1, k1] 5(3:4:7) times, p1, Tw2R, p1, [p1, k4, p2, Tw2R, p1] 1(2:2:2) times, [p1, k2] 5 times, p1, [p1, Tw2L, p2, k4, p1] 1(2:2:2) times, p1, Tw2L, p1, [k1, p1] 5(3:4:7) times, k1.
3rd row As 1st row.
4th row K1, [p1, k1] 5(3:4:7) times, p1, Tw2R, p1, [p1, C4B, p2, Tw2R, p1] 1(2:2:2) times, p1, k2, [p1, FC] twice, p1, [p1, Tw2L, p2, C4F, p1] 1(2:2:2) times, p1, Tw2L, p1, [k1, p1] 5(3:4:7) times, k1.
5th row As 1st row.
6th row As 2nd row.
7th row As 1st row.
8th row K1, [p1, k1] 5(3:4:7) times, p1, Tw2R, p1, [p1, C4B, p2, Tw2R, p1] 1(2:2:2) times, [p1, BC] twice, p1, k2, p1, [p1, Tw2L, p2, C4F, p1] 1(2:2:2) times, p1, Tw2L, p1, [k1, p1] 5(3:4:7) times, k1.
These last 8 rows form the patt and are repeated.
Work in patt until Back measures 19(21:23:24)cm/7½(8¼:9:9½)in from cast-on edge, ending with a WS row.
shape armholes
Cont in patt, cast/bind off 5 sts at beg of next 2 rows. 56(68:72:84) sts.**
Cont straight in patt until Back measures 30(33:36:38)cm/11¾(13:14:15)in from cast-on edge, ending with a WS row.
shape shoulder
Cast/bind off 13(19:20:26) sts at beg of next 2 rows, working 2 sts tog in centre of each 4-st cable.
Leave rem 30(30:32:32) sts on a holder for back neck.

front

Work as for Back to **.
Cont straight in patt until Front measures 25(28:33:35)cm/9¾(11:13:13¾)in from cast-on edge, ending with a WS row.

shape neck

Next row (RS) Patt 21(27:29:35) sts, turn and cont in patt on these sts only, leaving rem sts on a spare needle.
Cast/bind off 2 sts at beg of next and foll 1(1:2:2) alt rows, then dec 1 st at beg of next 4(4:3:3) alt rows. 13(19:20:26) sts.
Cont straight until Front matches Back to shoulder, ending with a WS row.
Cast/bind off, working 2 sts tog in centre of each 4-st cable.
With RS facing, slip 14 sts at centre front onto a holder, rejoin yarn to rem sts and patt to end.
Complete to match first side, reversing shaping.

sleeves

With 4½mm(US 7) needles and A, cast on 27(32:32:37) sts.
Change to M.
Work 6 rows in rib as for Back.
Inc row (RS) K and inc 5(0:4:3) sts evenly across row. 32(32:36:40) sts.
Change to 5mm(US 8) needles.
1st row (WS) [P1, k1] 2(2:3:4) times, k1, p2, k2, [p2, k1] 5 times, k1, p2, k1, [k1, p1] 2(2:3:4) times.
2nd row (RS) [P1, k1] 2(2:3:4) times, p1, Tw2R, p2, [k2, p1] 5 times, p1, Tw2L, p1, [k1, p1] 2(2:3:4) times.
These last 2 rows set the position of the central lattice cable with twist sts and moss/seed st to each side.
Cont in patt and working the lattice cable as for Back, inc 1 st at each end of 4th and every foll 4th row until there are 52(56:60:64) sts, taking all inc sts into moss/seed st.
Cont straight until Sleeve measures 18(21:24:28)cm/7(8¼:9½:11)in from cast-on edge.
Mark each end of last row, then work 6 rows more.
Cast/bind off in patt.

neckband

Join right shoulder seam.
With RS facing, 4½mm(US 7) needles and M, pick up and k 18 sts down left front neck, k across 14 sts at centre front, pick up and k 18 sts up right front neck, then k across 30(30:32:32) sts at centre back and inc 2(2:0:0) sts evenly. 82 sts.
1st rib row (WS) K2, [p3, k2] to end.
2nd rib row (RS) P2, [k3, p2] to end.
Rep last 2 rows twice more, then first rib row again.
Change to A and cast/bind off in patt.

to finish

Join left shoulder and neckband seam. Sew sleeves into armholes, joining row ends above markers to cast-/bound-off armhole stitches. Join side and sleeve seams.

multicolour bobble cardigan

This colourful cardigan was inspired by Mexican textiles. The bright bobbles decorating the neck, cuffs and hem will be irresistible to tiny fingers.

materials

4(5:5:6) 50g/1¾oz balls of King Cole *Anti-Tickle Merino DK* in main colour **M** (navy blue/Irish Navy 25) and small amount each in **A** (royal blue/Royal 21), **B** (mauve/Larkspur 13), **C** (yellow/Gold 55), **D** (red/Cherry 29) and **E** (hot pink/Raspberry 67) and **F** (jade/Green Ice 63)

Pair of 3¾mm(US 5) knitting needles

5(6:6:7) buttons

sizes

to fit

6–12 mths	1–2	2–3	3–4	yrs

actual measurements

chest

56	61	66	71	cm
22	24	26	28	in

length

30	33	36	38	cm
11¾	13	14	15	in

sleeve seam

18	21	23	28	cm
7	8¼	9	11	in

tension/gauge

23 sts and 32 rows to 10cm/4in over st-st using 3¾mm(US 5) needles

abbreviations

beg beginning; **cm** centimetre(s); **cont** continu(e)(ing); **dec** decrease; **foll** follow(s)(ing); **in** inch(es); **inc** increase; **k** knit; **p** purl; **patt** pattern; **rem** remaining; **rep** repeat; **RS** right side; **sl** slip; **st(s)** stitch(es); **st-st** stocking/stockinette stitch; **tog** together; **WS** wrong side; **yrn (yarn round needle)** wrap yarn around right needle from front to back and to front again between needles to make a st

back

With 3¾mm(US 5) needles and M, cast on
63(69:75:81) sts.
Moss/seed st row K1 [p1, k1] to end.
This last row forms moss/seed st and is repeated.
Work in 3cm/1¼in in moss/seed st.
Beg with a RS (k) row, work in st-st until back
measures 16(18:20:21)cm/6¼(7:7¾:8¼)in from cast-
on edge, ending with a WS (p) row.
shape armholes
Cast/bind off 3(4:5:6) sts at beg of next 2 rows.
57(61:65:69) sts.
Dec 1 st at each end of next and 3(4:4:5) foll RS rows.
49(51:55:57) sts.
Cont straight until Back measures
30(33:36:38)cm/11¾(13:14:15)in from cast-on edge,
ending with a WS row.
shape shoulders
Cast/bind off 8 sts at beg of next 4 rows.
Leave rem 17(19:23:25) sts on a holder.

pocket lining (make 1)

With 3¾mm(US 5) needles and M, cast on
15(17:19:21) sts.
Work 5(6:6:7)cm/2(2½:2½:2¾)in in st-st, ending with
a WS row.
Leave sts on a holder.

left front

With 3¾mm(US 5) needles and M, cast on
35(37:41:43) sts.
Work 3cm/1¼in in moss/seed st as for Back.
Next row (RS) K to last 5 sts, moss/seed st 5.
Next row (WS) Moss/seed st 5, p to end.
These last 2 rows set the position for the st-st with
moss/seed st button band and are repeated.
Work in patt as set until Front measures
8(8:10:10)cm/3¼(3¼:4:4)in from cast-on edge, ending
with a WS row.
place pocket
Next row (RS) K10(10:12:12), slip next
15(17:19:21) sts onto a holder for pocket top, k across
15(17:19:21) sts of pocket lining, k5, moss/seed st 5.
Cont in patt as set, work until Front measures

16(18:20:21)cm/6¼(7:7¾:8¼)in from cast-on edge,
ending with a WS row.
shape armhole
Cast/bind off 3(4:5:6) sts at beg of next row.
Work 1 row in patt.
Cont in patt, dec 1 st at armhole edge on next and
3(4:4:5) foll RS rows. 28(28:31:31) sts.
Cont straight in patt until Front measures
24(27:30:32)cm/9¼(10½:11¾:12½)in from cast-on
edge, ending with a WS row.
shape neck
Next row (RS) K to last 5 sts and slip these rem 5
moss/seed sts at front edge onto a safety pin for
neckband.
Cont in st-st, cast/bind off 2 sts at beg (neck edge) of
next and foll 1(1:2:2) alt row(s), then dec 1 st at beg
of foll 3(3:4:4) alt rows. 16 sts.
Cont straight until Front measures same as Back to
shoulder, ending with a WS row.
shape shoulder
Cast/bind off 8 sts at beg of next row and foll alt
row.
Mark the position for 5(6:6:7) buttons on the button
band, the first on the 3rd moss/seed st row after
cast-on, the last to come in the neckband and the rem
3(4:4:5) spaced evenly between.

right front

With 3¾mm(US 5) needles and M, cast on
35(37:41:43) sts.
Work 2 rows in moss/seed st as for Back.
Work first buttonhole on next row to match position
of first button marker as foll:
Buttonhole row (RS) K1, p2tog, yrn, [p1, k1] to
end.
Cont in moss/seed st until Front measures 3cm/1¼in
from cast-on edge.
Next row (RS) Moss/seed st 5, k to end.
Next row (WS) P to last 5 sts, moss/seed st 5.
These last 2 rows set the position for the st-st with
moss/seed st buttonhole band and are repeated.
Working buttonholes as before to match markers
throughout and cont in patt as set, work until Front
measures 16(18:20:21)cm/6¼(7:7¾:8¼)in from cast-
on edge, ending with a RS row.

shape armhole

Cast/bind off 3(4:5:6) sts at beg of next row.
Cont in patt, dec 1 st at armhole edge on next and
3(4:4:5) foll RS rows. 28(28:31:31) sts.
Cont straight in patt until Front measures
24(27:30:32)cm/9¼(10½:11¾:12½)in from cast-on
edge, ending with a RS row.

shape neck

Next row (WS) P to last 5 sts and slip these rem 5
moss/seed sts onto a safety pin for neckband.
Cont in st-st, cast/bind off 2 sts at beg (neck edge) of
next and foll 1(1:2:2) alt row(s), then dec 1 st at beg
of foll 3(3:4:4) alt rows. 16 sts.
Cont straight until Front measures same as Back to
shoulder, ending with a RS row.

shape shoulder

Cast/bind off 8 sts at beg of next row and foll alt row.

sleeves

With 3¾mm(US 5) needles and M, cast on
33(35:37:39) sts.
Work 3cm/1¼in in moss/seed st as for Back.
Inc row (RS) K and inc 6 sts evenly across row.
39(41:43:45) sts.
Beg with a WS (p) row and working in st-st, inc 1 st at
each end of 3rd and every foll 3rd row until there are
63(67:73:81) sts.
Cont straight in st-st until Sleeve measures
18(21:23:28)cm/7(8¼:9:11)in from beg, ending with
a WS row.

shape top

Cast/bind off 3(4:5:6) sts at beg of next 2 rows.
Dec 1 st at each end of next and 3(4:4:5) foll RS rows.
Cast/bind off rem 49(49:53:57) sts.

neckband

Join shoulder seams.
With WS facing, 3¾mm(US 5) needles and M,
moss/seed st across 5 sts of right front band, turn and
now with RS facing, moss/seed st 5, pick up and k 17
sts up right front neck, k across 17(19:23:25) sts from
back neck holder, pick up and k 17 sts down left front
neck, then moss/seed st across 5 sts of left front band.
61(63:67:69) sts.

Work 1 row in moss/seed st.
Buttonhole row (RS) K1, p2tog, yrn, moss/seed st
to end.
Work 4 rows more in moss/seed st.
Cast/bind off in moss/seed st.

pocket tops

With RS facing, 3¾mm(US 5) needles and M, work 4
rows in moss/seed st across 15(17:19:21) sts on
pocket top holder.
Cast/bind off in moss/seed st.

bobbles

Make several in each of six contrasting colours (A, B,
C, D, E and F) as foll:
With 3¾mm(US 5) needles, cast on 1 st.
1st row (RS) [K1, p1, k1, p1, k1] all into 1 st. 5 sts.
Beg with a p row, work 3 rows in st-st on these 5 sts.
5th row (RS) Pass 2nd, 3rd, 4th and 5th sts over first
st, then k into back of rem st.
Break yarn and pull through last st. Tie the two yarn
ends together to create the bobble.

to finish

Sew sleeves into armholes. Join side and sleeve seams.
Sew on buttons. Mixing the colours, sew bobbles to the
back, fronts and sleeves above the moss/seed-st edges,
and around the neck edge below moss/seed-st edge.

zip-up jacket

With it's chunky zip fastener and useful pockets, this multi-purpose jacket is ideal for playing outdoors and keeping found treasures safe.

materials

6(7:7:8) 50g/1¾oz balls of Debbie
    Bliss *Merino Aran* in red/Red 700
Pair of 5mm(US 8) knitting needles
25(25:30:30)/10(10:12:12)in open-
    ended zip fastener
6 small wooden buttons

sizes

to fit

6–12 mths	1–2	2–3	3–4	yrs

actual measurements

chest

56	61	66	71	cm
22	24	26	28	in

length

30	33	36	38	cm
11¾	13	14	15	in

sleeve seam (with cuff turned back)

18	21	23	28	cm
7	8¼	9	11	in

tension/gauge

18 sts and 32 rows to 10cm/4in over moss/seed stitch using 5mm(US 8) needles

abbreviations

beg beginning; **cm** centimetre(s); **cont** continu(e)(ing); **dec** decrease; **foll** follow(s)(ing); **in** inch(es); **inc** increase; **k** knit; **p** purl; **patt** pattern; **rem** remaining; **RS** right side; **st(s)** stitch(es); **st-st** stocking/stockinette stitch; **tbl** through back of loop(s); **tog** together; **WS** wrong side; **yo (yarn over needle)** take yarn over right needle to make a st; **yrn (yarn round needle)** wrap yarn around right needle from front to back and to front again between needles to make a st

back

With 5mm(US 8) needles, cast on 51(55:59:65) sts.
Moss/seed stitch row K1, [p1, k1] to end.
This last row forms moss/seed st and is repeated.
Working in moss/seed st throughout, cont until Back
measures 18(20:22:23)cm/7(8:8¾:9)in from cast-on
edge, ending with a WS row.

shape armholes

Cast/bind off 4(4:6:6) sts at beg of next 2 rows.
Cont straight until Back measures
30(33:36:38)cm/11¾(13:14:15)in from cast-on edge,
ending with a WS row.

shape shoulders

Cast/bind off 11(12:11:13) sts at beg of next 2 rows.
Leave rem 21(23:25:27) sts on a holder.

front pocket linings (make 2)

With 5mm(US 8) needles, cast on 11(13:13:15) sts.
Work 25(25:27:27) rows in moss/seed st.
Leave sts on a holder.

front pocket flaps (make 2)

With 5mm(US 8) needles, cast on 13(15:15:17) sts.
Work 2 rows in moss/seed st.
Buttonhole row K1, p1, k2tog, [yrn] twice, p2tog,
k1, [p1, k1] 0(1:1:2) times, p2tog, yrn, yo, k2tog, p1,
k1.
Next row [K1, p1] twice, k1tbl, [p1, k1] 2(3:3:4)
times, p1tbl, k1, p1, k1.
Work 1 row in moss/seed st.
Leave sts on a holder.

left front

With 5mm(US 8) needles, cast on 23(25:29:31) sts.
Working in moss/seed st throughout, work until
Front measures 9(9:11:11)cm/3½(3½:4¼:4¼)in from
cast-on edge, ending with a WS row.

place pocket

Next row (RS) Moss/seed st 6(6:8:8), cast/bind off
next 11(13:13:15) sts, moss/seed st to end.
Next row (WS) Moss/seed st 6(6:8:8), moss/seed st
across 11(13:13:15) sts of one pocket lining,
moss/seed st to end.

Next row (RS) Moss/seed st 5(5:7:7), holding pocket flap stitch holder at front of work, work pocket flap sts tog with next 13(15:15:17) sts of front, moss/seed st to end.

Cont straight until Front measures same as Back to armhole, ending with a WS row (a RS row for Right Front).

shape armhole

Cast/bind off 4(4:6:6) sts at beg of next row.

Cont straight until Front measures 25(27:30:31)cm/9¾(10½:11¾:12¼)in from cast-on edge, ending with a WS row (a RS row for Right Front).

shape neck

Next row Moss/seed st to last 3(4:5:5) sts and slip these rem 3(4:5:5) sts at Front edge onto a safety pin.

Work 2 rows in moss/seed st.

Cast/bind off 2 sts at beg (neck edge) of next row and 1 st at beg of foll 3(3:5:5) alt rows.

Work straight on rem 11(12:11:13) sts until Front matches Back to shoulder, ending with a WS row (a RS row for Right Front).

Cast/bind off in moss/seed st.

right front

Work as for Left Front, but noting exceptions in ( )s.

sleeve pocket lining (make 1)

With 5mm(US 8) needles, cast on 11 sts.

Work 17 rows in moss/seed st.

Leave sts on a holder.

sleeve pocket flap

With 5mm(US 8) needles, cast on 13 sts.

Work 2 rows in moss/seed st.

Buttonhole row K1, p1, k2tog, [yrn] twice, p2tog, k1, p2tog, yrn, yo, k2tog, p1, k1.

Next row [K1, p1] twice, k1tbl, [p1, k1] twice, p1tbl, k1, p1, k1.

Work 1 row in moss/seed st.

Leave sts on a holder.

left sleeve

With 5mm(US 8) needles, cast on 23(25:29:31) sts.

Work 26 rows in moss/seed st.

Cont in moss/seed st throughout, inc 1 st at each end of next and every foll 4th(4th:5th:6th) row, until there are 43(47:51:55) sts, taking inc sts into moss/seed st, **and at the same time** when Sleeve measures 16(19:21:26)cm/6¼(7½:8¼:10¼)in from cast-on edge, place the pocket lining and flap centrally over the next 3 rows as for Fronts.

When all sts have been increased, cont straight until Sleeve measures 22(25:27:32)cm/8½(9¾:10½:12½)in from cast-on edge.

Mark each end of last row, then work 7(7:10:10) rows more.

Cast/bind off.

right sleeve

Work as for Left Sleeve, but omitting pocket.

collar

Join shoulder seams.

With WS facing and 5mm(US 8) needles, moss/seed st across 3(4:5:5) sts on Right Front safety pin, turn, moss/seed st 3(4:5:5), pick up and k 15(17:17:20) sts up Right Front neck, moss/seed st across 21(23:25:27) sts on back neck holder, pick up and k 15(17:17:20) sts down Left Front neck, then moss/seed st across 3(4:5:5) sts on Left Front safety pin. 57(65:69:77) sts.

Work 15(15:17:17) rows in moss/seed st.

Cast/bind off.

to finish

Sew sleeves into armholes, joining row ends above markers to cast-/bound-off sts at underarm. Join sleeve seams. Join side seams, leaving lower 4cm/1½in open for side slits. Handstitch zip fastener to front edges. Slipstitch pocket linings in place. Sew buttons to pocket fronts to correspond with buttonholes.

robin hood jacket

This snuggly hooded jacket is perfect for keeping warm on cold autumn days. It is finished with wooden toggles and a cute tasseled hood.

materials

5(6:6:7) 50g/1¾oz balls of Rowan *Cork* in orange/Delight 040 or grey/Turbid 33
Pair each of 7mm(US 10½) and 7½mm(US 11) knitting needles
Cable needle
4 buttons or toggles

sizes

to fit

6–12 mths	1–2	2–3	3–4	yrs

actual measurements

chest

58	63	68	71	cm
23	25	27	28	in

length

30	33	36	38	cm
11¾	13	14	15	in

sleeve seam

18	21	23	27	cm
7	8¼	9	10¾	in

tension/gauge

16 sts and 23 rows to 10cm/4in over moss/seed st using 7½mm (US 11) needles

abbreviations

C4B (cable 4 back) sl next 2 sts onto cable needle and hold at back of work, k2, then k2 from cable needle; **C4F (cable 4 front)** as C4B, but hold cable needle in front of work; **cm** centimetre(s); **cont** continu(e)(ing); **Cr4L (cross 4 left)** sl next 2 sts onto cable needle and hold at front of work, p2, then k 2 from cable needle; **Cr4R (cross 4 right)** sl next 2 sts onto cable needle and hold at back of work, k2, then p2 from cable needle; **dec** decrease; **foll** follow(s)(ing); **in** inch(es); **inc** increase(e)(ing); **k** knit; **m1** make one st by picking up and working into back of loop lying between last st and next st; **p** purl; **patt** pattern; **rem** remaining; **rep** repeat; **RS** right side; **sl** slip; **st(s)** stitch(es); **tog** together; **WS** wrong side; **yrn (yarn round needle)** wrap yarn around right needle from front to back and to front again between needles to make a st

cable panel

Worked over a panel of 16 sts.

1st row (WS) P2, k4, p4, k4, p2.

2nd row (RS) K2, p4, C4F, p4, k2.

3rd and every foll WS row K all the k sts and p all p sts as they appear.

4th row Cr4L, p2, k4, p2, Cr4R.

6th row P2, Cr4L, C4F, Cr4R, p2.

8th row P4, C4B, C4B, p4.

10th row P2, Cr4R, C4F, Cr4L, p2.

12th row Cr4R, p2, k4, p2, Cr4L.

These 12 rows form the cable panel and are repeated in positions given in the instructions.

back

With 7mm(US 10½) needles, cast on 46(50:54:58) sts.

1st moss/seed st row (RS) [K1, p1] to end.

2nd moss/seed st row [P1, k1] to end.

Rep last 2 rows once more and first row again.

Inc row (WS) Moss/seed 2(4:2:4), m1, [moss/seed 2, m1] 1(1:3:3) times, moss/seed 3, m1, moss/seed 4, m1, moss/seed 2, m1, moss/seed 4, m1, moss/seed 3, [m1, moss/seed 2] 3 times, m1, moss/seed 3, m1, moss/seed 4, m1, moss/seed 2, m1, moss/seed 4, m1, moss/seed 3, [m1, moss/seed 2] 2(2:4:4) times, moss/seed 0(2:0:2). 62(66:74:78) sts.

Change to 7½mm(US 11) needles.

Foundation row (RS) P2(4:2:4), [k4, p2] 1(1:2:2) times, k2, p4, k4, p4, k2, p2, [k4, p2] twice, k2, p4, k4, p4, k2, [p2, k4] 1(1:2:2) times, p2(4:2:4).

1st row (WS) K2(4:2:4), [p4, k2] 1(1:2:2) times, work across 16 sts of first row of cable panel, k2, [p4, k2] twice, work across 16 sts of first row of cable panel, [k2, p4] 1(1:2:2) times, k2(4:2:4).

2nd row (RS) P2(4:2:4), [C4F, p2] 1(1:2:2) times, work 2nd row of cable panel, p2, [C4F, p2] twice, work 2nd row of cable panel, [p2, C4F] 1(1:2:2) times, p2(4:2:4).

3rd and every foll WS row K all the k sts and p all

p sts as they appear.

4th row (RS) P2(4:2:4), [k4, p2] 1(1:2:2) times, work 4th row of cable panel, p2, [k4, p2] twice, work 4th row of cable panel, [p2, k4] 1(1:2:2) times, p2(4:2:4).

These last 4 rows set the position of the cable panels and form the simple 4-st cables and are repeated, working the correct cable panel rows.

Work in patt until Back measures 30(33:36:38)cm/11¾(13:14:15)in from cast-on edge, ending with a RS row and noting the cable panel row.

Cast/bind off all sts, working 2 sts tog in centre of each cable.

left front

With 7mm(US 10½) needles, cast on 27(29:31:33) sts.

Moss/seed st row K1, [p1, k1] to end.

Rep last row 4 more times.

Inc row (WS) Moss/seed 5, m1, moss/seed 2, m1, moss/seed 3, m1, moss/seed 4, m1, moss/seed 2, m1, moss/seed 4, m1, moss/seed 3, m1, [moss/seed 2, m1] 1(1:3:3) times, moss/seed 2(4:2:4). 35(37:41:43) sts.

Change to 7½mm(US 11) needles.

Foundation row (RS) P2(4:2:4), [k4, p2] 1(1:2:2) times, k2, p4, k4, p4, k2, p2, k4, p1, [p1, k1] twice.

1st row (WS) [k1, p1] twice, k1, p4, k2, work across 16 sts of first row of cable panel, [k2, p4] 1(1:2:2) times, k2(4:2:4).

2nd row (RS) P2(4:2:4), [C4F, p2] 1(1:2:2) times, work 2nd row of cable panel, p2, C4F, p1, [p1, k1] twice.

3rd row [k1, p1] twice, k1, p4, k2, work 3rd row of cable panel, [k2, p4] 1(1:2:2) times, k2(4:2:4).

4th row P2(4:2:4), [k4, p2] 1(1:2:2) times, work 4th row of cable panel, p2, k4, p1, [p1, k1] twice.

These last 4 rows set the position of the cable panel with moss/seed-st front border and form the simple 4-st cables and are repeated, working the correct cable panel rows.

Work in patt, ending 9 rows below Back, so ending with a WS row.

shape neck

Next row (RS) Patt to last 10 sts, turn, leave these 10 sts on a holder for hood and cont on rem

25(27:31:33) sts.

Dec 1 st at neck edge on next 7 rows.

Work 1 row.

Cast/bind off all sts, working 2 sts tog in centre of each cable.

Mark the position for 4 buttons on the front border, the first to be worked on the 3rd row after cast-on, the last just below neck shaping and the rem 2 spaced evenly between.

right front

With 7mm(US 10½) needles, cast on 27(29:31:33) sts.

Moss/seed st row K1, [p1, k1] to end.

Rep last row once more.

Buttonhole row (RS) K1, p1, yrn, p2tog, k1, [p1, k1] to end.

Work 2 rows in moss/seed st.

Inc row (WS) Moss/seed 2(4:2:4), m1, [moss/seed 2, m1] 1(1:3:3) times, moss/seed 3, m1, moss/seed 4, m1, moss/seed 2, m1, moss/seed 4, m1, moss/seed 3, m1, moss/seed 2, m1, moss/seed 5.

Change to 7½mm(US 11) needles.

Foundation row (RS) [K1, p1] twice, p1, k4, p2, k2, p4, k4, p4, k2, [p2, k4] 1(1:2:2) times, p2(4:2:4).

1st row (WS) K2(4:2:4), [p4, k2] 1(1:2:2) times,

work 16 sts of first row of cable panel, k2, p4, k1, [p1, k1] twice.

2nd row (RS) [K1, p1] twice, p1, C4F, p2, work 2nd row of cable panel, [p2, C4F] 1(1:2:2) times, p2(4:2:4).

3rd row K2(4:2:4), [p4, k2] 1(1:2:2) times, work 3rd row of cable panel, k2, p4, k1, [p1, k1] twice.

4th row [K1, p1] twice, p1, k4, p2, work 4th row of cable panel, [p2, k4] 1(1:2:2) times, p2(4:2:4).

These last 4 rows set the position of the cable panel with moss/seed-st front border and form the simple 4-st cables and are repeated, working the correct cable panel rows.

Working buttonholes as before on RS rows to match markers, work in patt, ending 9 rows below Back, so ending with a WS row.

shape neck

Next row (RS) Patt 10 sts and slip these onto a holder for hood, patt to end.

Dec 1 st at neck edge on next 7 rows.

Work 1 row.

Cast/bind off all sts, working 2 sts tog in centre of each cable.

sleeves

With 7mm(US 10½) needles, cast on 22(22:26:26) sts.

1st moss/seed st row (RS) [K1, p1] to end.

2nd moss/seed st row [P1, k1] to end.

Rep last 2 rows once more and first row again.

Inc row (WS) Work in moss/seed st and inc 10(10:12:12) sts evenly across row. 32(32:38:38) sts.

Change to 7½mm(US 11) needles.

Foundation row (RS) Moss/seed st 1(1:4:4) sts, p1, k4, p2, k2, p4, k4, p4, k2, p2, k4, p1, moss/seed st 1(1:4:4) sts.

1st row (WS) Moss/seed st 1(1:4:4) sts, k1, p4, k2, work across 16 sts of first row of cable panel, k2, p4, k1, moss/seed st 1(1:4:4) sts.

2nd row (RS) Moss/seed st 1(1:4:4) sts, p1, C4F, p2, work 2nd row of cable panel, p2, C4F, p1, moss/seed st 1(1:4:4) sts.

3rd row Moss/seed st 1(1:4:4) sts, k1, p4, k2, work 3rd row of cable panel, k2, p4, k1, moss/seed st 1(1:4:4) sts.

4th row Moss/seed st 1(1:4:4) sts, p1, k4, p2, work

4th row of cable panel, p2, k4, p1, moss/seed st 1(1:4:4) sts.

These last 4 rows set the position of the cable panel and 4-st cables with moss/seed st to each side and are repeated, working correct cable panel rows.

Working in patt as set, inc 1 st at each end of next RS row and every foll 6th row until there are 42(44:50:52) sts, taking inc sts into moss/seed st.

Cont straight in patt until Sleeve measures 18(21:23:27)cm/7(8¼:9:10¾)in from cast-on edge, ending with a RS row.

Cast/bind off, working 2 sts tog in centre of each cable.

hood

Join shoulder seams.

With RS facing and 7mm(US 10½) needles, slip 10 sts from Right Front holder onto needle, pick up and k 10 sts up Right Front neck, 27 sts across Back neck, and 10 sts down Left Front neck, then patt across 10 sts on Left Front holder. 67 sts.

1st row (WS) [K1, p1] twice, k1, p4, k1, [p1, k1] 5 times, moss/seed across 27 sts of Back neck and inc 8 sts evenly, [k1, p1] 5 times, k1, p4, k1, [p1, k1] twice.

This last row sets the position of the moss/seed and cable border with moss/seed st between.

Cont straight in patt as set, keeping the cables correct until hood measures 21(24:27:29)cm/ 8¼(9½:10¾:11½)in from cast-on edge.

Cast/bind off.

to finish

Fold cast/bound-off edge of hood in half and join seam. Matching centre of cast/bound-off edge of sleeve to shoulder seam, sew on sleeves. Join side and sleeve seams. Sew on buttons. Make a tassel and sew to hood point.

fun to wear

funky tank top

This cotton top looks great in bright colours or muted tones. Experiment with your own colourways to find a combination that will suit your own funky monkey.

materials

2 50g/1¾oz balls of Rowan *Handknit DK Cotton* in **A** (blue/Galaxy 308 or brown/Tope 253) and one ball each in **B** (red/Rosso 215 or sea green/Nautical 311), **C** (orange/Flame 254 or light sea green/Ice Water 239), **D** (yellow/Sunflower 304 or off-white/Ecru 251), **E** (lime green/Gooseberry 219 or green/Foggy 301) and **F** (turquoise/Oasis 202 or beige/Linen 205)
Pair each of 3¾mm(US 5) and 4mm(US 6) knitting needles

tension/gauge

20 sts and 28 rows to 10cm/4in over st-st using 4mm(US 6) needles

abbreviations

beg beginning; **cm** centimetre(s); **cont** continu(e)(ing); **dec** decrease; **foll** follow(s)(ing); **in** inch(es); **k** knit; **p** purl; **patt** pattern; **rem** remaining; **rep** repeat; **RS** right side; **sl** slip; **st(s)** stitch(es); **st-st** stocking/stockinette stitch; **tog** together; **WS** wrong side

sizes

to fit

6–12 mths	1–2	2–3	3–4	yrs

actual measurements

chest

56	61	66	71	cm
22	24	26	28	in

length

30	33	36	38	cm
11¾	13	14	15	in

stripe sequence

12 rows B, 9 rows C, 8 rows A, 3 rows D, 9 rows E,
7 rows F, 8 rows C, 6 rows B, 9 rows D, 4 rows A,
10 rows F, 10 rows E

back

With 3¾mm(US 5) needles and A, cast on
56(60:66:70) sts.
1st row (RS) K2(0:2:0), p2(1:2:1), [k3, p2]
10(11:12:13) times, k2(3:2:3), p0(1:0:1).
2nd row (WS) P2(0:2:0), k2(1:2:1), [p3, k2]
10(11:12:13) times, p2(3:2:3), k0(1:0:1).
Rep last 2 rows 4(4:5:5) times more and first row
again, so ending with a RS row.
P 1 row.
Change to 4mm(US 6) needles and B.
Beg with a RS (k) row, work 38(44:48:52) rows in
st-st in stripe sequence.
shape armholes
Keeping stripe sequence correct, cast/bind off
4(4:5:5) sts at beg of next 2 rows, then dec 1 st at
each end of next row and 3 foll RS rows. 40(44:48:52)
sts.**
Cont straight in striped st-st for 23(25:29:31) rows
more.
shape back neck
Next row (RS) K10(11:12:14), turn and cont on
these sts only, leaving rem sts on a spare needle.
Cast/bind off 2 sts at beg of next row.
Cast/bind off rem 8(9:10:12) sts.
With RS facing, slip 20(22:24:24) sts at centre back
onto a holder, rejoin yarn to rem sts and k to end.
P 1 row.
Cast/bind off 2 sts at beg of next row.
Cast/bind off rem 8(9:10:12) sts.

front

Work as for Back to **.
Cont straight in striped st-st for 11(13:17:19) rows
more.
shape front neck
Next row (RS) K15(16:17:19), turn and cont on
these sts only, leaving rem sts on a spare needle.
Cast/bind off 2 sts at beg (neck edge) of next and foll

WS row, then dec 1 st at beg of 3 foll WS rows.
8(9:10:12) sts.
Work 4 rows more.
Cast/bind off.
With RS facing, slip 10(12:14:14) sts at centre front
onto a holder, rejoin yarn to rem sts and complete to
match first side, reversing shaping.

neckband

Join right shoulder.
With RS facing, 3¾mm(US 5) needles and A, pick up
and k 14 sts down left front neck, k across
10(12:14:14) sts at centre front, pick up and k 14 sts
up right front neck, 2 sts at right back neck, k across
20(22:24:24) sts at centre back, then pick up and k 2
sts up left back neck. 62(66:70:70) sts.
1st row (WS) P2(1:0:0), [k2, p3] 12(13:14:14)
times.
2nd row (RS) [K3, p2] 12(13:14:14) times,
k2(1:0:0).
Rep last 2 rows twice more.
Cast/bind off in patt.

armbands

Join left shoulder and neckband seam.
With RS facing, 3¾mm(US 5) needles and A, pick up
and k 72(76:86:90) sts around armhole edge.
1st row (WS) K2(0:0:1), p3(2:2:3), [k2, p3]
13(14:16:17) times, k2(2:2:1), p0(2:2:0).
2nd row (RS) P2(0:0:1), k3(2:2:3), [p2, k3]
13(14:16:17) times, p2(2:2:1), k0(2:2:0).
Rep last 2 rows once more.
Cast/bind off in patt.

to finish

Join side and armband seams.

sundress

This knitted dress is cool to wear and stylish too. Its bold design was inspired by a day at the seaside – striped deckchairs and old-fashioned swimming costumes.

materials

2(3:3:3) 50g/1¾oz balls of Rowan *Cotton Glacé* in main colour **M** (red/ Poppy 741) and 2 balls in **A** (off-white/Ecru 725)
Pair each of 2¾mm(US 2) and 3¼mm(US 3) needles
2 buttons

sizes

to fit

| 6–12 mths | 1–2 | 2–3 | 3–4 | yrs |

actual measurements

chest at underarm

| 56 | 61 | 65 | 70 | cm |
| 22 | 24 | 26 | 28 | in |

length to shoulder (adjustable)

| 41 | 45 | 49 | 53 | cm |
| 16 | 17¾ | 19¼ | 20¾ | in |

tension/gauge

23 sts and 32 rows to 10cm/4in over st-st using 3¼mm(US 3) needles

abbreviations

alt alternate; **beg** begin(ning); **cm** centimetre(s); **cont** continu(e)(ing); **dec** decrease; **foll** follow(s)(ing); **in** inch(es); **k** knit; **p** purl; **rem** remaining; **rep** repeat; **RS** right side; **sl** slip; **ssk** sl 1 knitwise, sl 1 knitwise, insert tip of left needle through fronts of both slipped sts and k2tog through back of loops; **st(s)** stitch(es); **st-st** stocking/ stockinette stitch; **tog** together; **WS** wrong side

back and front (both alike)

With 2¾mm(US 2) needles and M, cast on
91(99:105:113) sts.
Moss/seed st row K1, [p1, k1] to end.
This row forms moss/seed st and is repeated.
Work 3cm/1¼in in moss/seed st.
Change to 3¼mm(US 3) needles.
Beg with a RS (k) row work in 8-row st-st stripe
repeat of 4 rows C, 4 rows M.
Work 4 rows, so ending with a WS (p) row in C.
Keeping st-st stripe sequence (4 rows C, 4 rows M)
correct throughout, beg shaping on next row as foll:
Dec row (RS) K5, ssk, k to last 7 sts, k2tog, k5.
Work 5 rows.
Rep last 6 rows 11(12:13:14) times more, so ending
with a WS row. 67(73:77:83) sts.
shape yoke
Cast/bind off 5(5:6:6) sts at beg of next 2 rows and
4(5:4:5) sts at beg of foll 2 rows, so ending with a WS
row. 49(53:57:61) sts.
Next row (RS) K1, ssk, k to last 3 sts, k2tog, k1.
Work 1 row.
Rep last 2 rows, 3 times more.
Work 2 rows.
Next row (RS) K1, ssk, k to last 3 sts, k2tog, k1.
Work 1 row.
Rep last 4 rows, 3(4:5:6) times more, so ending with a
WS row.
Work 4 rows.
Leave rem 33(35:37:39) sts on a holder.

armhole edging

Join side seams, matching stripes.
With RS facing, 2¾mm(US 2) needles and M, pick up
and k 79(85:91:103) sts around armhole edge.
Work 4 rows in moss/seed st.
Cast/bind off purlwise while working p1, then [p2tog,
p1] to end.

front yoke edging

With RS facing, 2¾mm(US 2) needles and M, pick up
and k 3 sts across row ends of armhole edging, k across
33(35:37:39) sts on front holder, then pick up and k 3
sts across row ends of armhole edging. 39(41:43:45)
sts.
Work 4 rows in moss/seed st.
Cast/bind off purlwise while working p1, then [p2tog,
p1] to end.

back yoke edging and straps

With RS facing, 2¾mm(US 2) needles and M, pick up
and k 3 sts across row ends of armhole edging, k across
33(35:37:39) sts on back holder, then pick up and k 3
sts across row ends of armhole edging. 39(41:43:45)
sts.
Work 5 rows in moss/seed st.
divide for straps
Next row (RS) Moss/seed st 18(19:20:21), work
2tog, turn and cont on these 19(20:21:22) sts only,
leaving rem sts on a spare needle.
**Dec 1 st at beg of next and 7(8:7:8) foll alt rows.
11(11:13:13) sts.
Cont straight in moss/seed st until strap measures
6(7:8:9)cm/2½(2¾:3¼:3½)in (adjust length here to
suit), ending with a WS row.
1st buttonhole row (RS) Moss/seed st 3(3:4:4),
cast/bind off 3 sts, moss/seed st to end.
2nd buttonhole row Work in moss/seed st and cast
on 3 sts over cast-/bound-off sts in previous row.
Work 4 rows more in moss/seed st.
Cast/bind off in moss/seed st.**
With RS facing, rejoin yarn to rem sts and moss/seed
st to end.
Work 1 row in moss/seed st.
Work as first strap from ** to **.

to finish

Sew buttons to front yoke to match buttonholes.

pirate sweater

An eye-catching skull and crossbones sweater will be a firm favourite with any would-be pirate.

materials

3(3:4:4) 50g/1¾oz balls of Rowan *Handknit DK Cotton* in main colour **M** (navy blue/Turkish Plum 277) and 2 balls each in **A** (red/Rosso 215) and **B** (off-white/Ecru 251)
Pair each of 3 ¾mm(US 5) and 4mm(US 6) knitting needles

sizes

to fit

6–12 mths	1–2	2–3	3–4	yrs

actual measurements

chest

56	61	66	71	cm
22	24	26	28	in

length

30	33	36	38	cm
11¾	13	14	15	in

sleeve seam

18	21	23	28	cm
7	8¼	9	11	in

tension/gauge

20 sts and 28 rows to 10cm/4in over st-st using 4mm(US 6) needles

abbreviations

alt alternate; **beg** beginning; **cm** centimetre(s); **cont** continu(e)(ing); **dec** decrease; **foll** follow(s)(ing); **in** inch(es); **inc** increase; **k** knit; **p** purl; **rem** remaining; **rep** repeat; **RS** right side; **st(s)** stitch(es); **st-st** stocking/stockinette stitch; **WS** wrong side

note

When working from chart, use separate small balls of yarn for motif, twisting yarns at colour change to avoid holes.

back

With 3¾mm(US 5) needles and M, cast on 56(60:66:70) sts.

Change to A and k 1 row.

Now work in rib as foll:

1st rib row (WS) P1(1:2:2), k2, [p2, k2] to last 1(1:2:2) sts, p1(1:2:2).

2nd rib row (RS) K1(1:2:2), p2, [k2, p2] to last 1(1:2:2) sts, k1(1:2:2).

Rep last 2 rows until rib measures 3(4:4:5)cm/1¼(1½:1½:2)in from cast-on edge, ending with a 1st rib row.**

Change to 4mm(US 6) needles and M.***

Beg with a RS (k) row, work 72(78:84:90) rows in st-st, so ending with a WS row.

shape back neck

Next row (RS) K16(17:20:21) sts, turn and cont on these sts only, leaving rem sts on a spare needle.

Cont in st-st, cast/bind off 2 sts at beg of next row.

Cast/bind off rem 14(15:18:19) sts.

With RS facing, slip 24(26:26:28) sts at centre onto a holder, rejoin yarn to rem sts and k to end.

P 1 row.

Cont in st-st, cast/bind off 2 sts at beg of next row.

Cast/bind off rem 14(15:18:19) sts.

front

Work as for Back to ***.

Beg with a RS (k) row, work 8(12:14:18) rows in st-st, so ending with a WS (p) row.

place motif

Next row (RS) K5(7:10:12)M, k across 46 sts of first row of chart, k5(7:10:12)M.

Cont in st-st foll chart until all 50 chart rows have been worked.

Cont in st-st in M only, work 2(4:8:10) rows.

shape neck

Next row (RS) K22(23:26:27) sts, turn and cont on these sts only, leaving rem sts on a spare needle.

****Cast/bind off 3 sts at beg (neck edge) of next row, 2 sts at beg of foll 2 alt rows and then dec 1 st at beg of next alt row. 14(15:18:19) sts.

Work 6 rows.

Cast/bind off.

With RS facing, slip 12(14:14:16) sts at centre front

onto a holder, rejoin yarn to rem sts and k to end.
P 1 row.
Complete as first side from **** to end.

sleeves

With 3¾mm(US 5) needles and B, cast on
24(28:30:34) sts.
Change to M and work rib as for Back from ** to **.
Change to 4mm(US 6) needles and A.
Beg with a RS (k) row, work in 16-row st-st stripe
repeat of 8 rows A, 8 rows B **and at the same time**
inc 1 st at each end of every foll 3rd(3rd:4th:4th) row
until there are 48(50:54:56) sts.
Cont straight in stripes as set until sleeve measures
18(21:23:28)cm/7(8¼:9:11)in from cast-on edge,
ending with a WS row.
Cast/bind off.

neckband

Join right shoulder seam.
With RS facing, 3¾mm(US 5) needles and B, pick up
and k 15 sts down left front neck, k across
12(14:14:16) sts at centre front, pick up and k 16 sts
up right front neck, 2 sts down right back neck, k
across 24(26:26:28) sts at back neck and dec 1 st in
centre, then pick up and k 2 sts up left back neck.
70(74:74:78) sts.
1st rib row (WS) P2, [k2, p2] to end.
2nd rib row (RS) K2, [p2, k2] to end.
Rep last 2 rows twice more, then first row again.
Cast/bind off in M.

to finish

Join left shoulder and neckband seam. Matching centre
of cast/bound-off edge of sleeve to shoulder, sew on
sleeves. Join side and sleeve seams.

skull and crossbones chart

key
☐ B
■ M

strawberries & cream sweater

The inspiration for this sweater is a classic summer dessert, strawberries and cream. The cream cotton knit features a pretty border of strawberries and vivid red edging.

materials

5(6:7) 50g/1¾oz balls of Rowan *Handknit DK Cotton* in main colour **M** (off-white/Ecru 251), one ball in **A** (red/Rosso 215) and small amount each in **B** (navy blue/Turkish plum 277) and **C** (lime green/Gooseberry 219)
Pair each of 3¾mm(US 5) and 4mm(US 6) knitting needles

sizes

to fit

1–2	3–4	5–6	yrs

actual measurements

chest

69	76	82	cm
27	30	32¼	in

length

36	41	47	cm
14¼	16¼	18½	in

sleeve seam

22	28	31	cm
8½	11	12	in

tension/gauge

20 sts and 28 rows to 10cm/4in over st-st using 4mm(US 6) needles

abbreviations

alt alternate; **beg** beginning; **cm** centimetres; **cont** continu(e)(ing); **dec** decrease; **foll** follow(s)(ing); **in** inch(es); **inc** increase; **k** knit; **p** purl; **rem** remaining; **rep** repeat; **RS** right side; **st(s)** stitch(es); **st-st** stocking/stockinette stitch; **WS** wrong side

note

When working zigzag patt from charts, strand yarn not in use across WS of work. When working motifs from charts, use separate small balls of A, B and C, twisting yarns at colour change to avoid holes. Do not work part motifs on 1st size.

back

**With 3¼mm(US 5) needles and A, cast on 68(76:84) sts.
Change to M and k 1 row.
Rib row [K2, p2] to end.
Rep last row 8 times more.
Change to 4mm(US 6) needles and beg with a RS (k) row, work 21 rows in st-st from strawberry border chart, so ending with a RS (k) row.
Beg with a p row and cont in st-st in M only, work 39(43:49) rows more, so ending with a WS row.
shape armholes
Cast/bind off 4(5:5) sts at beg of next 2 rows. 60(66:74) sts.**
Cont straight for 32(40:52) rows more, so ending with a WS row.
shape back neck
Next row (RS) K19(21:24), turn and p to end.
Cast/bind off.
With RS facing, slip centre 22(24:26) sts onto a holder, rejoin yarn to rem sts and k to end.
P 1 row.
Cast/bind off.

front

Work as for Back from ** to **.
Cont straight for 20(26:36) rows more, so ending with a WS row.
shape front neck
Next row (RS) K26(29:32), turn and cont on these sts only, leaving rem sts on a spare needle.
Cast/bind off 3 sts at beg of next row.
Dec 1 st at neck edge on next 4(2:3) rows, then dec 1 st at neck edge on foll 0(3:2) alt rows. 19(21:24) sts.
Cont straight for 8(6:9) rows more.
Cast/bind off.
With RS facing, slip 8(8:10) sts at centre front onto a holder, rejoin yarn to rem sts and k to end.
P 1 row.
Cast/bind off 3 sts at beg of next row.
Dec 1 st at neck edge on next 4(2:3) rows, then dec 1 st at neck edge on foll 0(3:2) alt rows. 19(21:24) sts.
Cont straight for 7(5:8) rows more.
Cast/bind off.

sleeves

With 3¾mm(US 5) needles and A, cast on 36(38:40) sts.

Change to M and k 1 row.

1st and 3rd sizes only

Work 7 rows in rib as for Back.

2nd size only

1st rib row K2, [p2, k2] to end.

2nd rib row P2 [k2, p2] to end.

Rep last 2 rows twice more and then first rib row again.

Change to 4mm(US 6) needles and beg with a RS (k) row, work 21 rows in st st from sleeve chart **and at the same time** inc 1 st at each end of 5th and every foll 4th row as shown, then work in M only and cont to inc as before until there are 60(68:80) sts.

Cont straight for 11(11:5) rows more.

Cast/bind off.

neckband

Join right shoulder.

With RS facing, 3¾mm(US 5) needles and M, pick up and k 18(20:21) sts down left front neck, k across 8(8:10) sts at centre front, pick up and k 18(20:21) sts up right front neck, 2 sts down right back neck, k across 22(24:26) sts at centre back and pick up and k 2 sts up left back neck. 70(76:82) sts.

Work in 5 rows in k2, p2 rib as for 2nd size sleeve. Change to A and rib 1 row as set, then cast/bind off using a 4mm(US 6) needle.

to finish

Join left shoulder and neckband seam. Matching centre of cast/bound-off edge of sleeve to shoulder, sew sleeve into armhole. Join side and sleeve seams.

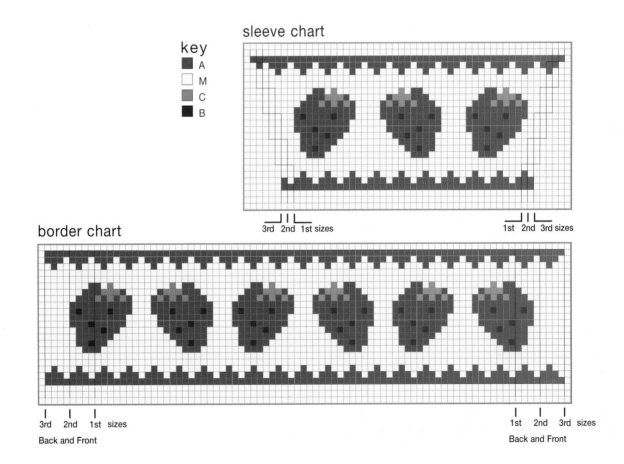

key
- A
- M
- C
- B

sleeve chart

3rd 2nd 1st sizes   1st 2nd 3rd sizes

border chart

3rd 2nd 1st sizes   1st 2nd 3rd sizes

Back and Front   Back and Front

heart-motif cardigan

Every little girl will love this cardigan. The contrast-edged frilled detailing gives it the perfect finish.

materials

5(5:6:6) 50g/1¾oz balls of Rowan *Handknit DK Cotton* in main colour **M** (blue/Diana 287) and one ball each in **A** (pink/Sugar 303), **B** (lilac/Lupin 305), **C** (orange/Flame 251), **D** (red/Rosso 215), **E** (yellow/Sunshine 304) and **F** (lime green/Lush 306)

Pair each of 3¾mm(US 5) and 4mm(US 6) knitting needles

5 buttons

sizes

to fit

6–12 mths	1–2	2–3	3–4	yrs
actual measurements				
chest				
56	61	66	71	cm
22	24	26	28	in
length				
30	33	36	38	cm
11¾	13	14	15	in
sleeve seam				
18	21	23	26	cm
7	8	9	10	in

tension/gauge

20 sts and 28 rows to 10cm/4in over st-st using 4mm(US 6) needles

abbreviations

alt alternate; **beg** beginning; **cm** centimetre(s); **cont** continu(e)(ing); **dec** decrease; **foll** follow(s)(ing); **in** inch(es); **inc** increase; **k** knit; **p** purl; **patt** pattern; **psso** pass slipped st over; **rem** remaining; **rep** repeat; **RS** right side; **skpo** sl 1, k1, psso; **sl** slip; **sts** stitch(es); **st-st** stocking/stockinette stitch; **tog** together; **WS** wrong side; **yrn (yarn round needle)** wrap yarn around right needle from front to back and to front again between needles to make a st

note

When working from charts, use a separate small ball of yarn for each motif, twisting yarns at colour change to avoid holes. When working sleeves, do not work incomplete heart motifs.

back

With 4mm(US 6) needles and A, cast on
140(152:162:180) sts.
Change to M.
1st row (WS) P.
2nd row (RS) P2(3:3:2), [skpo, k3, k2tog, p3] to
last 8(9:9:8) sts, skpo, k3, k2tog, p1(2:2:1).
3rd row K all k sts and p all p sts.
4th row P2(3:3:2), [skpo, k1, k2tog, p3] to last
6(7:7:6) sts, skpo, k1, k2tog, p1(2:2:1).
5th row As 3rd row.
6th row P2(3:3:2), [sl 1, k2tog, psso, p3] to last
4(5:5:4) sts, sl 1, k2tog, psso, p1(2:2:1).
7th row K1(2:2:1), [p1, k3] to last 3(4:4:3) sts, p1,
k2(3:3:2). 56(62:66:72) sts.
Beg with a RS (k) row and starting on chart row
5(3:1:1), work in st-st from chart, working between
lines for correct size.
Cast/bind off sts for armhole and back neck shaping
where shown, and cast/bind off back neck sts.

pocket lining (make 1)

With 4mm(US 6) needles and M, cast on
15(17:17:19) sts.
Beg with a RS (k) row, work 20(20:22:22) rows in
st-st.
Leave sts on a holder.

left front

With 4mm(US 6) needles and A, cast on
79(88:90:99) sts.
Change to M.
1st row (WS) P.
2nd row (RS) P2(1:3:2), [skpo, k3, k2tog, p3] to
last 7sts, skpo, k3, k2tog.
3rd row K all k sts and p all p sts.
4th row P2(1:3:2), [skpo, k1, k2tog, p3] to last 5
sts, skpo, k1, k2tog.
5th row As 3rd row.
6th row P2(1:3:2), [sl 1, k2tog, psso, p3] to last 3
sts, sl 1, k2tog, psso.
7th row (WS) [P1, k3] to last 3(2:4:3) sts, p1,
k2(1:3:2). 31(34:36:39) sts.
Next row (RS) K26(29:31:34), [k1, p1] twice, k1.

Next row (WS) K1, [p1, k1] twice, p to end.
These last 2 rows set the position for the st-st with moss/seed st button band.
Keeping the st-st and moss/seed st as set, work from chart (only the st-st areas are shown) until 20(20:22:22) st-st chart rows have been worked.
place pocket
Next row (RS) K8(9:11:12), slip next 15(17:17:19) sts onto a holder for pocket top, k across 15(17:17:19) sts of pocket lining, k3, moss/seed st 5.
Cont to work from chart until chart row 68(74:80:86) has been worked.
shape neck
Next row (RS) Patt to last 5 sts and slip these rem 5 moss/seed sts onto a safety pin.
Complete foll chart, working neck shaping as shown.
Mark the position of 5 buttons on the moss/seed st button band, the first directly above the lower frill, the last just below the neck shaping and the rem 3 spaced evenly between.

right front

With 4mm(US 6) needles and A, cast on 79(88:90:99) sts.
Change to M.
1st row (WS) P.
2nd row (RS) [Skpo, k3, k2tog, p3] to last 9(8:10:9) sts, skpo, k3, k2tog, p2(1:3:2).
3rd row K all k sts and p all p sts.
4th row [Skpo, k1, k2tog, p3] to last 7(6:8:7) sts, skpo, k1, k2tog, p2(1:3:2).
5th row As 3rd row.
6th row [Sl 1, k2tog, psso, p3] to last 5(4:6:5) sts, sl 1, k2tog, psso, p2(1:3:2).
7th row (WS) K2(1:3:2), p1, [k3, p1] to end. 31(34:36:39) sts.
Buttonhole row (RS) K1, p1, yrn, p2tog, k1, k to end.
Next row (WS) P to last 5 sts, [k1, p1] twice, k1.
Next row (RS) K1, [p1, k1] twice, k to end.
The last 2 rows set the position for the st-st with moss/seed-st buttonhole band.
Keeping the st-st and moss/seed st as set, work from chart (only the st-st areas are shown), working buttonholes on RS rows as before, to match button markers, until chart row 69(75:81:87) has been worked.

Next row (WS) Patt to last 5 sts and slip rem 5 moss/seed-sts onto a safety pin.
Complete foll chart, working neck shaping as shown.

sleeves

With 4mm(US 6) needles and A, cast on 75(75:85:85) sts.
Change to M.
1st row (WS) P.
2nd row (RS) P4, [skpo, k3, k2tog, p3] to last st, p1.
3rd row K all k sts and p all p sts.
4th row P4, [skpo, k1, k2tog, p3] to last st, p1.
5th row As 3rd row.
6th row P4, [sl 1, k2tog, psso, p3] to last st, p1.
7th row (WS) K1, [k3, p1] to last 4 sts, k4. 33(33:37:37) sts.
Beg with a RS (k) row on chart row 3(1:1:1) and working in st-st from chart within lines for correct size, inc 1 st at each end of 5th(7th:7th:7th) row, then on foll 4th and 6th rows alternately for 1st and 2nd sizes only and every foll 6th row for 3rd and 4th sizes only, until there are 49(51:55:57) sts.
Cont straight until chart row 46(52:56:64) has been worked.
Mark each end of last row, then work 6 rows more.
Cast/bind off.

pocket top

With RS facing, 3¾mm(US 5) needles and M, k across 15(17:17:19) sts of pocket.
Work 4 rows in moss/seed st.
Cast/bind off in moss/seed st.

collar

Join shoulder seams.
With WS facing, 3¾mm(US 5) needles and M, moss/seed st across 5 sts on safety pin at right front.
Next row (RS) Cast/bind off 2 sts, moss/seed st rem 2 sts, pick up and k 16(16:17:17) sts up right front neck, 22(24:26:28) sts around back neck, 17(17:18:18) sts down left front neck, then moss/seed st across 5 sts on left front safety pin.
Next row (WS) Cast/bind off 2 sts, moss/seed st to end. 61(63:67:69) sts.
Cont in moss/seed st until collar measures 2cm/¾in.
Change to 4mm(US 6) needles and work 5cm/2in more in moss/seed st.
Cast/bind off in moss/seed st.

to finish

Sew sleeves into armholes, joining row ends above markers to cast-/bound-off sts at underarm. Join side, sleeve and edging seams. Slipstitch pocket lining and top in place.

sleeve chart

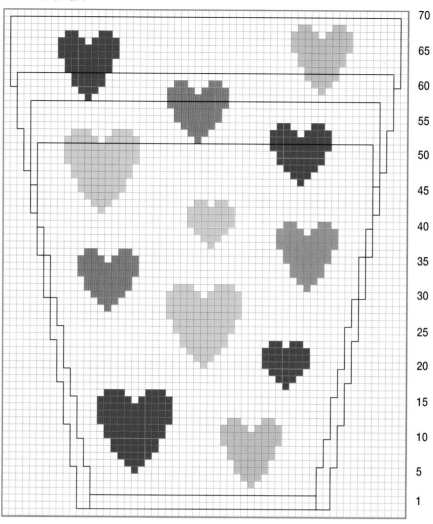

back and front chart

key

F
C
E
A
B
D
M

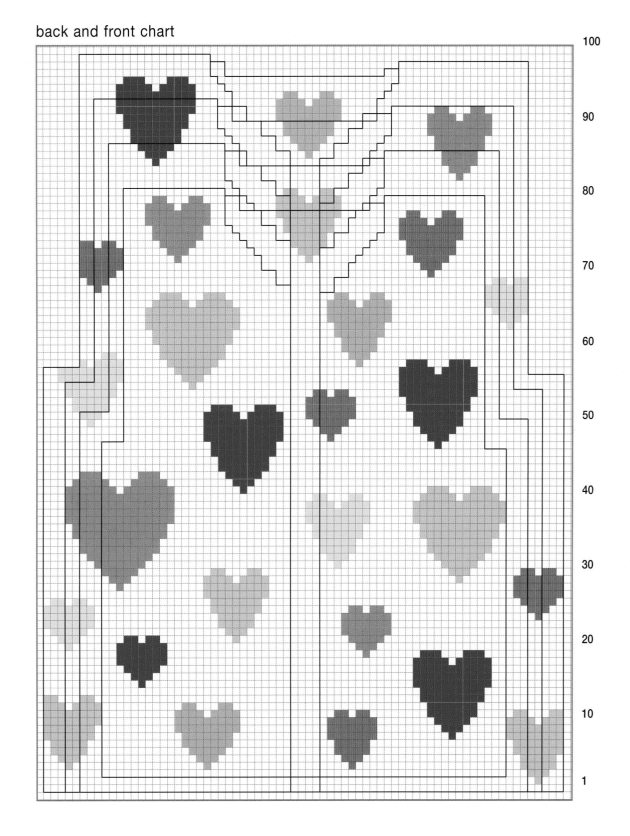

100

90

80

70

60

50

40

30

20

10

1

fairy dress

What could be more fun than being a fairy or princess?
The simple bodice with pretty ribbon ties and net skirt
make this the ideal outfit for every special occasion.

materials

1(1:2:2) 50g/1¾oz balls of Jaeger
   Aqua in main colour **M** (hot pink/
   India 322) and one ball in **A** (lilac/
   Comfrey 328)
Pair of 3¾mm(US 5) knitting needles
   3¾mm(US 5) circular needle
1m/1yd each of dark pink, pale pink
   and lilac net fabric
2m/2yd of 15mm-/½in-wide pink
   ribbon
waist length of 5mm-/¼in-wide
   elastic
Sewing thread

sizes

to fit

6–12 mths	1–2	3–4	4–5	yrs

actual measurements

chest

45	54	57	61	cm
17¾	21¼	22½	24	in

tension/gauge

22 sts and 30 rows to 10cm/4in
over st-st using 3¾mm(US 5) needles

abbreviations

alt alternate; **beg** beginning; **cm**
centimetre(s); **cont** continu(e)(ing);
dec decrease; **foll** follow(s)(ing);
in inch(es); **k** knit; **p** purl; **patt**
pattern; **rem** remaining; **RS** right
side; **st(s)** stitch(es); **st-st**
stocking/stockinette stitch; **tog**
together; **WS** wrong side

bodice back

With 3¾mm (US 5) needles and A, cast on
49(59:63:67) sts.
K 1 row.
Change to M and work in patt as foll:
1st row (RS) K12(15:16:17), p1, [k1, p1]
12(14:15:16) times, k12(15:16:17).
2nd row (WS) P12(15:16:17), k1, [p1, k1]
12(14:15:16) times, p12(15:16:17).
These last 2 rows form the patt and are repeated.
Cont in patt until bodice back measures
13(14:15:16)cm/5(5½:6:6¼)in from cast-on edge,
ending with a WS row.
shape armhole
Cast/bind off 3(3:4:4) sts at beg of next 2 rows and
2 sts at beg of foll 2(6:6:6) rows, then dec 1 st at each
end of next and foll 2(1:1:2) alt rows. 33(37:39:41)
sts.
P 1 row.
shape neck
Next row (RS) K7, turn and cont on these sts only,
leaving rem sts on a spare needle.
Cast/bind off 3 sts at beg (neck edge) of next row and
2 sts at beg of foll alt row. 2 sts.
K1 row.
P2tog and fasten off.
With RS facing, slip 19(23:25:27) sts at centre onto a
holder, rejoin yarn to 7 rem sts and complete to match
first side.

bodice front

With 3¾mm(US 5) needles and A, cast on
49(59:63:67) sts.
K 1 row.
Change to M and work as for Back, but in st-st only.

edging

Join right side seam.
With RS facing, 3¾mm(US 5) circular needle and A,
pick up and k 18(22:23:25) sts up left front armhole
edge, 8 sts down left front neck, k across 19(23:25:27)
sts at centre front, pick up and k 8 sts up right front
neck, 36(44:46:50) sts around right armhole edge, 8
sts down right back neck, k across 19(23:25:27) sts at
centre back, then pick up and k 8 sts up left back neck
and 18(22:23:25) sts down left back armhole edge.
142(166:174:186) sts.
Cast/bind off knitwise.
Join left side seam. Cut ribbon into four lengths and
stitch to back and front of the bodice.

skirt

Following the illustration below, cut the net into petal
shapes. Place the layers over each other and fold the
straight edges over, running a line of stitching along to
hold them in place. Thread elastic through the hem to
form a skirt and stitch the ends of elastic together.
Then stitch to the lower edge of the bodice.

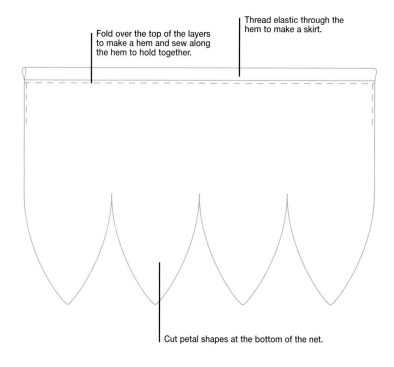

Fold over the top of the layers
to make a hem and sew along
the hem to hold together.

Thread elastic through the
hem to make a skirt.

Cut petal shapes at the bottom of the net.

luxury lettered coat

A bold woolly knit that is great fun to wear and educational, too! Have fun helping your child find their own initials or spell out the letters in their name.

materials

2 balls of Rowan *Yorkshire Tweed DK* main colour **M** (bright blue/Slosh 345) and 1 ball in each of (red/Scarlet 344), (purple/Revel 342), (dark blue/Champion 346), (green/Frog 349), (yellow/Lime Leaf 348), (turquoise/Skip 347) and (pale pink/Frolic 350)
Pair each of 3mm(US 2–3) and 3¾mm(US 5) knitting needles
5 buttons

sizes

to fit

6–12 mths	1–2	2–3	yrs
actual measurements			
chest			
56	63	70	cm
22	24¾	27½	in
back length			
32	37	41	cm
12½	14½	16	in
sleeve seam			
15	19	21.5	cm
6	7½	8½	in

tension/gauge

23 sts and 32 rows to 10cm/4in over st-st using 3¾mm(US 5) needles

abbreviations

cm centimetre(s); **foll(s)** follow(s)(ing); **in** inch(es); **k** knit; **k2tog** knit next 2 sts together; **mm** millimetre(s); **p** purl; **st(s)** stitch(es); **st-st** stocking/stockinette stitch; **yo (yarn over needle)** take yarn over right needle to make a st

note

When working from chart, use separate small balls of yarn for each colour area and twist yarns at colour change to avoid holes.

back

With 3mm(US 2–3) needles and M, cast on 64(72:80) sts.

1st row *K, p1, rep from * to end.
2nd row *P1, k1, rep from * to end.
Work 6 rows more in moss/seed st.
Change to 3¾mm(US 5) needles and st-st.
Using intarsia method, foll chart.

left front

With 3mm(US 2–3) needles and M, cast on 32(36:40) sts.
Work 8 rows in moss/seed st as given for back.
Change to 3¾mm(US 5) needles and st-st.
Using intarsia method, foll chart.

right front

Work as given for Left Front, foll the correct chart.

sleeves

With 3mm(US 2–3) needles and M, cast on 32(34:34) sts.
Work 8 rows in moss/seed st as given for back.
Change to 3¾mm(US 5) needles and st-st.
Using intarsia method, foll chart.

button band

With 3mm(US 2–3) needles and M, cast on 6 sts.
Work in moss/seed st as given for back until band, when slightly stretched, fits from cast on edge to neck of Left Front.
Cast/bind off.
Sew Button Band to Left Front.
Mark positions for 5 buttons, the first 1cm/¾in from cast-on edge, the fifth 1cm/¾in from top of band, the rem 3 evenly spaced between.

buttonhole band

Work as for Button Band, making buttonholes as moss/seed st 2 sts, k2tog, yo, moss/seed 2 sts, where marked on Button Band.
Sew band to Right Front.

collar

Join shoulder seams.
With 3mm(US 2–3) needles and M, and starting and finishing halfway across front bands, pick up and k 22(25:26) sts from right front neck, 24(26:28) sts from back neck and 22(25:26) sts from left front neck. 68(76:80).
Work 6cm/2¼in in moss/seed stitch as given for back.
Cast/bind off loosely.

to finish

Pin sleeves to body, centre of sleeve top to shoulder seam and stitch. Join underarm and side seams. Weave in loose ends. Sew on buttons.

lettered coat chart: size 1

key
- M
- red
- purple
- dark blue
- green
- yellow
- pale pink

size 1 sleeve

size 1 sleeve

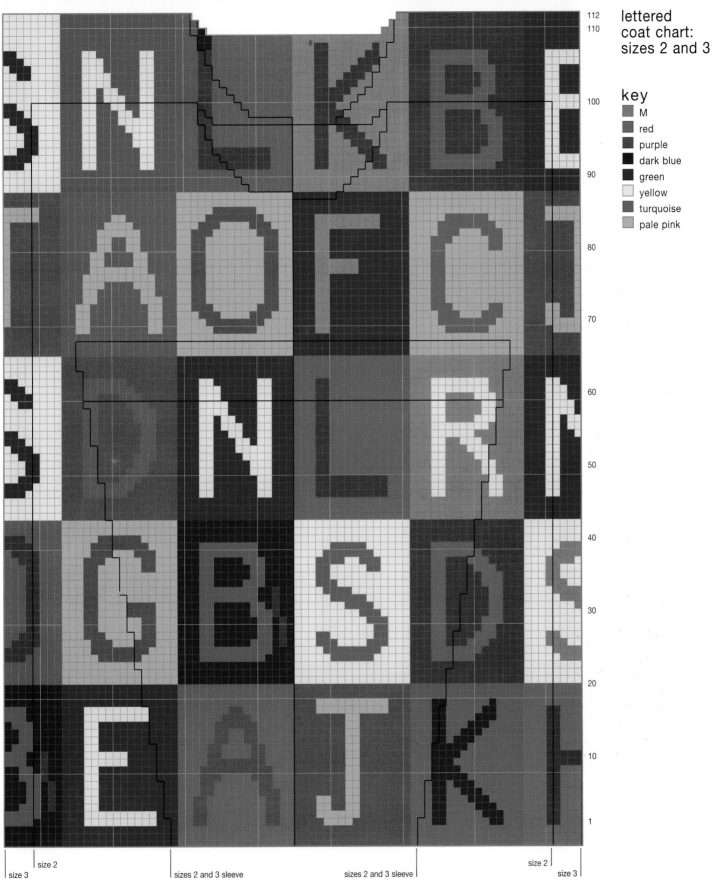

key

M
red
purple
dark blue
green
yellow
turquoise
pale pink

size 3
size 2
sizes 2 and 3 sleeve
sizes 2 and 3 sleeve
size 2
size 3

head honcho poncho

This stripy poncho is eye-catching and fun to wear. The simple design makes it easy to take on and off and it's very fashionable, too.

materials

2(3:4) Jaeger *Matchmaker Merino DK* in (orange/Pumpkin 898) and 2(3:4) in (pink/Rock Rose 896), 2(2:2) in (blue/Pacific 889), 2(2:2) in (purple/Azalea 897)

2(2:2) Jaeger *Baby Merino DK* in (red/Red 231) and 2(2:2) in (yellow/Gold 225)

Pair each of 3¼mm(US 3) and 3¾mm(US 5) knitting needles

Spare knitting needle

Crochet hook

1 button

sizes

To fit

6–12 mths	1–2	2–3	yrs
actual measurements			
chest			
51	55	61	cm
20	21½	24	in
back length			
32	37	41	cm
12½	14½	16	in
wingspan			
61	76	85	cm
24	30	33½	in

tension/gauge

23 sts and 32 rows to 10cm/4in over st-st using 3¾mm(US 5) needles

abbreviations

alt alternate; **beg** begin(ning); **cm** centimetre(s); **cont** continue; **dec** decreas(e)(ing); **foll(s)** follow(s)(ing); **inc** increas(e)(ing); **in** inch(es); **k** knit; **k2tog** knit next 2 sts together; **mm** millimetre; **p** purl; **p2tog** purl next 2 sts together; **patt** pattern; **PM** place marker(s); **psso** pass slipped stitch over; **rem** remain(ing); **rep** repeat; **RS** right side; **skpo** s1, k1, psso; **s1** slip next stitch; **st(s)** stitch(es); **st-st** stocking/stockinette stitch; **WS** wrong side; **yo (yarn over needle)** take yarn over right needle to make a st

back and front (both alike)

With 3¾mm(US 5) needles and orange, cast on 192(228:264) sts.

1st row *K1, p1, rep from * to end.

2nd row *P1, p1, rep from * to end.

Cont in moss/seed st as follows:

3rd row *Dec, moss/seed st 92(110:128), dec, rep from * once. 188(224:260) sts.

4th and alternate rows Moss/seed st without shaping.

5th row *Dec, moss/seed st 90(108:126), dec, rep from * once. 184(220:256) sts.

7th row *Dec, moss/seed st 88(106:124), dec, rep from * once. 180(216:252) sts.

9th row *Dec, moss/seed st 86(104:122), dec, rep from * once. 176(212:248) sts.

11th row *Dec, moss/seed st 84(102:120), dec, rep from * once. 172(208:244) sts.

Change to Pink and st-st.

Place 5 markers on last row - first marker between centre 2 sts, leave 29(35:41) sts then place first pair of markers, leave a further 29(35:41) sts then place 2nd pair of markers, leaving 28(34:40) sts at row-end edges beyond markers.

13th row K2tog, k to within 2 sts of 3rd (centre) marker, skpo, slip marker onto right needle, k2tog, k to last 2 sts, skpo. 168(204:240) sts.

14th row P.

15th row K2tog, [k to within 2 sts of next marker, skpo, slip marker onto right needle] 3 times, [k2tog, k to next marker, slip marker onto right needle] twice, k2tog, k to last 2 sts, skpo. 160(196:232) sts.

16th row P.

17th to 20th rows As 13th and 14th rows, twice. 152 (188:224) sts.

13th to 20th rows form patt.

Using Pink, patt 4 rows more. 140(176:212) sts.

Change to Red and patt 12 rows. 112(148:184) sts.

Change to Yellow and patt 12 rows. 80(116:152) sts.

Change to Blue and patt 12 rows. 52(88:124) sts.

Change to Purple and patt 8(12:12) rows. 32(56:92) sts.

sizes 2 and 3 only

Change to Orange and patt (8:12) rows. (36:64) sts.

size 3 only

Change to Pink and patt 8 rows. 44 sts.

all sizes

Break yarn and leave sts on a holder.

neckband

Join right shoulder seam.

With RS facing, 3 1/4mm (US 3) needles and Purple (Orange:Pink), k 32(36:44) sts from front holder, then 32(36:44) sts from back holder. 64(72:88) sts.

1st row K3, *p2, k2, rep from * to last st, k1.

2nd row K1, *p2, k2, rep from * to last 3 sts, p2, k1.

Rep 1st and 2nd rows twice more.

Cast/bind off loosely in rib.

Join left shoulder seam, leaving 7cm/2 3/4in open at neck edge.

With RS facing, 3 1/4mm (US 3) needles and same colour as used for Neckband, pick up and k 30 sts around opening.

Next row (buttonhole row) K2, k2tog, yfwd, k to end.

Cast/bind off knitways.

to finish

Sew on button. Weave in any loose ends.

fringe

Cut yarns into 15cm/6in lengths. With 3 lengths together, fold in half and, using a crochet hook, pull fold through cast-on knitting. Pull the ends through the loop and pull tight. Attach fringe around cast-on edge of poncho at intervals and in colours of your choice.

angel dress

A delightful dress that will make every little girl look like an angel. It feels gorgeous in sumptuous silk and is great for christenings, weddings or any other special occasion.

materials

3(3) 50g/1¾oz balls Jaeger *Silk* in pale blue/Blue Lily 128
Pair each of 2¾mm(US 2) and 3mm(US 2–3) knitting needles
Circular 2¾mm(US 2) knitting needle
1 small button

sizes

to fit

3–6	9–12	mths

actual measurements

chest

47	52	cm
18½	20½	in

length to shoulder

36	41	cm
14	16	in

tension/gauge

28 sts and 38 rows to 10cm/4in over st-st using 3mm(US 2–3) needles

abbreviations

alt alternate; **beg** begin(ning); **cm** centimetre(s); **cont** continue; **dec** decreas(e)(ing); **foll(s)** follow(s)(ing); **in** inch(es); **k** knit; **k2tog** knit next 2 sts together; **mm** millimetre; **p** purl; **psso** pass slipped stitch over; **rem** remain(ing); **rep** repeat; **RS** right side; **s1** slip one stitch; **skpo** s1, k1, psso; **st(s)** stitch(es); **st-st** stocking/stockinette stitch; **WS** wrong side; **yo (yarn over needle)** take yarn over right needle to make a st

back

**With 3mm(US 2–3) needles, cast on 124(132) sts.
K 2 rows.
Beg with a k row, work 6(8) rows in st-st.
Dec row (RS) K13(14), skpo, k to last 15(16) sts,
k2tog, k13(14).
Work 5(7) rows in st-st.
Rep the last 6(8) rows until 100(110) sts rem.
Cont straight until back measures 23(27)cm/9(10½)in
from cast-on edge, ending with a p row.
Dec row (RS) K3(5), [k2tog, k1] 32(34) times,
k1(3). 68(76) sts.
Cont in st-st without shaping until back measures
26(30)cm/10¼(11¾)in from cast-on edge, ending with
a p row.

shape armholes
Cast/bind off 6 sts at beg of next 2 rows. 56(64) sts.
Cast/bind off 5 sts at beg of next 2 rows. 46(54) sts.
Dec 1 st at each end of the next row and every foll alt
row until 36(42) sts rem.
P 1 row.**

back opening
Next row (RS) K17(20), turn and work on these sts
only for first side of back opening.
Next row Cast on 2 sts, k these 2 sts, then p to end.
19(22) sts.
Cont in st-st with 2 sts at centre back worked as k2 on
every row, until back measures 33(38)cm/13(15)in from
cast-on edge, ending with a p row.
shape neck
Next row (RS) K to last 7(9) sts, leave these sts on a
holder, turn.
Cont in st-st dec 1 st at neck edge on every row until 6(8)
sts rem.
Cont straight until back measures 36(41)cm/14¼(16)in
from cast-on edge, ending with a p row.
shape shoulder
Cast/bind off.
With RS facing, rejoin yarn to rem sts, k to end.
Cont in st-st with 2 sts at centre back worked as k2 on
every row, until back measures 33(38)cm/13(15)in from
cast-on edge ending with a p row.
shape neck
Next row (RS) K7(9), leave sts on a holder, k to end.
Cont in st-st dec 1 st at neck edge on every row until 6(8)
sts rem.
Cont straight until back measures 36(41)cm/14¼(16)in
from cast-on edge, ending with a p row.
shape shoulder
Cast/bind off.

front

Work as given for Back from ** to **.
shape neck
Next row (RS) K13(15) sts, turn and work on these sts
only for first side of neck shaping.
Dec 1 st at neck edge on every foll alt row until 6(8) sts
rem.
Cont without further shaping until front measures same
as Back to Shoulder, ending at side edge.
shape shoulder
Cast/bind off.
With RS facing, slip centre 10(12) sts onto a holder,
rejoin yarn to rem sts, k to end.
Complete to match first side, reversing shaping.

neckband

Join shoulder seams.
With RS facing and 2¾mm(US 2) circular needle, slip 7(9) sts from left back onto needle, pick up and k 11 sts up left back to shoulder, k 25(28) sts down left front neck, k across 10(12) sts from front neck holder, pick up and k 25(28) sts up right front neck to shoulder, k 11 sts from right back neck, k across 7(9) sts on back neck holder. 96(108) sts.
Work backwards and forwards in rows.
K 1 row.
Next row (buttonhole row) K1, yf, k2tog, k to end.
Next row (picot cast/bind-off row) (WS) Working knitwise, cast/bind off 3 sts, *slip st from right needle back onto left needle, cast on 2 sts, cast/bind off 5 sts: rep from * to end.

armbands

Join left shoulder and neckband seam.
With RS facing and 2¾mm(US 2) needles, pick up and k 84(88) sts evenly around armhole edge.
K 2 rows.
Cast/bind off knitwise.

lower edging

Join left side and armband seam. With RS facing and 2¾mm(US 2) circular needle, pick up and k 246(262) sts around lower edge of back and front.
Next row (picot cast/bind-off row) (WS) Working knitwise, cast/bind off 2 sts, *slip st from right needle back onto left needle, cast on 2 sts, cast/bind off 5 sts, rep from * to end, ending the last rep with cast/bind-off rem sts.

to finish

Join right side and armband seam. Overlap bands at centre back opening. Sew on button.

ballerina wrap

This ballerina wrap can be jazzed up with a colourful ribbon or toned down with a plain tie. Either way, it looks great worn with a pretty skirt.

materials

3(4:4:4) 50g balls of Debbie Bliss *Baby Cashmerino* in pale blue/Pale Blue 202

Pair each of 3mm(US 2) and 3¼mm(US 3) knitting needles

1m/1yd of 2cm-/¾in-wide ribbon

sizes

to fit

6–12 mths	1–2	2–3	3–4	yrs

actual measurements

chest

56	61	66	71	cm
22	24	26	28	in

length

23	25	28	31	cm
9	9¾	11	12	in

sleeve seam

18	21	23	28	cm
7	8¼	9	11	in

tension/gauge

25 sts and 34 rows to 10cm/4in over st-st using 3¼mm(US 3) needles

abbreviations

beg beginning; **cm** centimetre(s); **cont** continu(e)(ing); **dec** decrease; **foll** follow(s)(ing); **in** inch(es); **inc** increase; **k** knit; **m1** make one st by picking up and working into back of loop lying between last st and next st; **p** purl; **rem** remaining; **rep** repeat; **RS** right side; **sl** slip; **st(s)** stitch(es); **st-st** stocking/stockinette stitch; **tog** together; **WS** wrong side

back

With 3mm(US 2) needles, cast on 57(65:69:73) sts.
K 2 rows.
Change to 3¼mm(US 3) needles.
Beg with a RS (k) row, work 8 rows in st-st, so ending
with a WS (p) row.
Inc row (RS) K2, m1, k to last 2 sts, m1, k2.
Con in st-st, work 5(5:7:7) rows.
Rep last 6(6:8:8) rows 4 times more. 67(75:79:83) sts.
Work 0(4:0:6) rows.
shape armholes
Cast/bind off 4(4:5:5) sts at beg of next 2 rows.
59(67:69:73) sts.
Work 38(42:46:50) rows.
shape shoulders
Cast/bind off 9(10:10:11) sts at beg of next 2 rows
and 8(10:10:10) sts at beg of foll 2 rows.
Leave rem 25(27:29:31) sts on a holder.

left front

With 3mm(US 2) needles, cast on 50(58:62:66) sts.
K 2 rows.
Change to 3¼mm(US 3) needles.
Beg with a RS (k) row, work 4 rows in st-st.
shape front slope
Next row (RS) K to last 3 sts, k2tog, k1.
P 1 row.
Rep last 2 rows once more.
Cont in st-st, dec 1 st at front edge as set on every foll
RS row and inc 1 st at side edge as for Back on next
row and 4 foll 6th(6th:8th:8th) rows.
Cont as set until 38(44:45:46) sts rem, ending with a
WS row.
shape armhole
Next row (RS) Cast/bind off 4(4:5:5) sts, k to last 3
sts, k2tog, k1.
Keeping armhole edge straight, cont to dec 1 st at
front edge on every foll RS row until 17(20:20:21) sts
rem.
Cont straight for 7(5:9:13) rows, so ending with a WS
row.
shape shoulders
Cast/bind off 9(10:10:11) sts at beg of next row.
P 1 row.
Cast/bind off rem 8(10:10:10) sts.

right front

With 3mm(US 2) needles, cast on 50(58:62:66) sts.
K 2 rows.
Change to 3¼mm(US 3) needles.
Beg with a RS (k) row, work 4 rows in st-st.
shape front slope
Next row (RS) K1, k2tog, k to end.
P 1 row.
Rep last 2 rows once more.
Cont in st-st, dec 1 st at front edge as set on every foll RS row and inc 1 st at side edge as for Back on next row and 4 foll 6th(6th:8th:8th) rows.
Cont as set until 37(43:44:45) sts rem, ending with a RS row.
shape armhole
Next row (WS) Cast/bind off 4(4:5:5) sts, p to end.
Keeping armhole edge straight, cont to dec 1 st at front edge on every foll RS row until 17(20:20:21) sts rem.
Cont straight for 8(6:10:14) rows, so ending with a RS row.
shape shoulders
Cast/bind off 9(10:10:11) sts at beg of next row.
K 1 row.
Cast/bind off rem 8(10:10:10) sts.

sleeves

With 3mm(US 2) needles, cast on 38(38:42:42) sts.
K 2 rows.
Change to 3¼mm(US 3) needles.
Beg with a RS (k) row, work 4 rows in st-st.
Inc row (RS) K2, m1, k to last 2 sts, m1, k2.
Cont in st-st, work 3 rows.
Rep last 4 rows until there are 58(64:70:74) sts.
Cont straight until sleeve measures 18(21:23:28)cm/7(8¼:9:11)in from cast-on edge, ending with a RS row.
Mark each end of last row, then work 5(5:7:7) rows more.
Cast/bind off.

front edging

Join shoulder seams.
With RS facing and 3mm(US 2) needles, pick up and

k 80(88:98:108) sts up right front edge, k across 25(27:29:31) sts at back neck, then pick up and k 80(88:98:108) sts down left front edge.
185(203:225:247) sts.
K 2 rows.
Cast/bind off knitwise.

to finish

Sew sleeves into armholes, joining row ends above sleeve markers to cast-/bound-off sts of armholes. Join sleeve seams. Join side seams, leaving a 2cm/¾in gap in left seam 1cm/⅛in above cast-on edge. Sew a 40cm/16in length of ribbon to right front edge below start of front slope shaping and rem 60cm/24in to left front edge.

heads, toes
& little hands

fair isle tassel hat

This cute hat with fun tassels will keep little heads warm and cosy. The bright Fair Isle design will brighten up even the darkest winter day.

materials

One 50g/1¾oz ball each of King Cole *Anti-Tickle Merino DK* in **A** (hot pink/Raspberry 67), **B** (baby pink/Dusky Pink 94), **C** (blue/Bluebell 26), **D** (light blue/Sky 5) and **E** (cream/Aran 46)

Pair of size 3¼mm(US 3) and 4mm(US 6) knitting needles

sizes

to fit

6–12 mths 1–2   2–3   3–4 yrs

tension/gauge

25 sts and 26 rows to 10cm/4in over patterned st-st using 4mm (US 6) needles

abbreviations

beg beginning; **cm** centimetre(s); **in** inch(es); **k** knit; **p** purl; **RS** right side; **st(s)** stitch(es); **st-st** stocking/stockinette stitch; **WS** wrong side

to make

With 3¼mm(US 3) needles and A, cast on
45(53:57:61) sts.

Moss/seed st row K1, [p1, k1] to end.

This row forms moss/seed st and is repeated.
Work 7(7:8:8)cm/2¾(2¾:3¼:3¼)in in moss/seed st.
Change to 4mm(US 6) needles.
Beg with a RS (k) row, work
10(11:12:13)cm/4(4¼:4¾:5)in in st-st from chart,
ending with WS row and noting the chart row.
With A, k 3 rows.
Beg with the same noted WS (p) chart row, work
10(11:12:13)cm/4(4¼:4¾:5)in in st-st from chart,
working back down the chart and ending with the first
chart row.
Change to 3¼mm(US 3) needles and A.
P 1 row.
Work 7(7:8:8)cm/2¾(2¾:3¼:3¼)in in moss/seed st.
Cast/bind off.

to finish

Fold the hat in half across the middle along the central
ridge row, matching the cast-on and cast-/bound-off
edge. Join the side seams.

Make 2 tassels in A, by winding yarn around your
fingers about 24 times. Cut the yarn. Thread a short
length through the loops and tie to hold the loops
together. Wind another short length around the loops
about 1cm/½in below the tied top and secure. Cut
through the lower end of the loops, so making the
tassel. Sew tassels to the top corners of the hat.

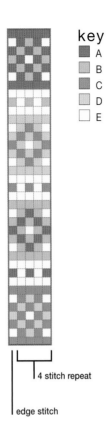

key

- A
- B
- C
- D
- E

4 stitch repeat

edge stitch

striped hat & scarf set

Little ones need to keep extra warm on cold days, so why not knit this trendy hat and scarf set to keep your child warm and looking great too?

materials

One 50g/1¾oz ball each of King Cole *Anti-Tickle Merino DK* in **A**, **B**, **C**, **D** and **E** (see *Note*)
Pair each of 3¼mm(US 3) and 3¾mm(US 5) knitting needles
Long 3¼mm(US 3) circular needle (for scarf only)

sizes

Hat

small   medium   large

Scarf

Approximately 92cm/36in by 16cm/6¼in

tension/gauge

23 sts and 32 rows to 10cm/4in over st-st using 3¾mm(US 5) needles

abbreviations

beg beginning; **cont** continu(e)(ing); **cm** centimetre(s); **foll** follow(s)(ing); **in** inch(es); **inc** increase; **k** knit; **p** purl; **patt** pattern; **rem** remaining; **rep** repeat; **RS** right side; **st(s)** stitch(es); **st-st** stocking/stockinette stitch; **tog** together; **WS** wrong side

note

Choose colours from the foll:
For **A**, turquoise/Turquoise 18 or yellow/Gold 55.
For **B**, cream/Aran 46.
For **C**, hot pink/Raspberry 67 or blue/Bluebell 26
For **D**, baby pink/Dusky Pink 94 or turquoise/Turquoise 18
For **E**, mauve/Larkspur 13 or light orange/Amber 10

earflaps for hat (make 2)

Using 3¾mm(US 5) needles and A, cast on 7(9:11) sts.
Beg with a RS (k) row and working in 20-row st-st
stripe repeat of 4 rows A, 4 rows B, 4 rows C, 4 rows
D, 4 rows E, shape flaps as foll:
Inc 1 st at each end of first, 2nd, 4th, 5th, and 7th
rows. 17(19:21) sts.
Work straight for 7(9:11) rows more.
Leave sts on a spare needle.

main hat

With RS of earflaps facing, 3¾mm(US 5) needles and
colour to keep earflap stripe patt correct as set on
earflaps, cast on 12(14:17) sts, k across 17(19:21) sts

of one earflap, cast on 32(36:44) sts, k across
17(19:21) sts of rem earflap, then cast on 12(14:17)
sts. 90(102:120) sts.
Beg with a WS (p) row and cont in st-st stripe patt as
set, work 19(20:23) rows more.
2nd size only
Next row (WS) P2tog, p to last 2 sts, p2tog.
90(100:120) sts.
all sizes
K 1 row.
shape top
Shape top of hat as foll:
1st row (WS) [P2tog, p8] to end.
K 1 row, then p 1 row.
4th row (RS) [K7, k2tog] to end.
P 1 row, then k 1 row.
7th row (WS) [P2tog, p6] to end.
K 1 row, then p 1 row.
10th row (RS) [K5, k2tog] to end. 54(60:72) sts.
1st size only
11th row [P2tog, p4] to end. 45 sts.
12th row [K3, k2tog] to end. 36 sts.
13th row [P2tog, p2] to end. 27 sts.
14th row [K2tog, k1] to end. 18 sts.
15th row [P2tog] to end. 9 sts.
16th row [K2tog] 4 times, k1. 5 sts.
Break yarn, thread through rem 5 sts, pull up and
secure.
2nd size only
P 1 row.
12th row (RS) [K4, k2tog] to end. 50 sts.
P 1 row.
14th row [K3, k2tog] to end. 40 sts.
P 1 row.
16th row [K2, k2tog] to end. 30 sts.
17th row [P1, p2tog] to end. 20 sts.
18th row [K2tog] to end. 10 sts.
P 1 row.
20th row [P2tog] to end. 5 sts.
Break yarn, thread through rem 5 sts, pull up and
secure.
3rd size only
P 1 row.
12th row (RS) [K4, k2tog] to end. 60 sts.
P 1 row.
14th row [K3, k2tog] to end. 48 sts.

P 1 row.

16th row [K2, k2tog] to end. 36 sts.

P 1 row.

18th row [K1, k2tog] to end. 24 sts.

P 1 row.

20th row [K2tog] to end. 12 sts.

21st row [P2tog] to end. 6 sts.

22nd row [K2tog] to end. 3 sts.

Break yarn, thread through rem 3 sts, pull up and secure.

edging for hat

With RS facing, 3¼mm(US 3) needles and C, pick up and k 12(14:17) sts across cast-on sts, 36(40:44) sts around right earflap, 32(36:44) sts across front cast-on sts, 36(40:44) sts around left earflap and 12(14:17) sts across cast-on sts. 128(144:166) sts.

K 2 rows.

Cast/bind off knitwise.

to finish hat

Join back seam. Cut six 60cm/24in lengths of C. Thread three of the lengths through the centre of the edging of each earflap. Taking three pairs of yarn lengths, make a plait/braid, knot the ends and trim.

to make scarf

With 3¼mm(US 5) needles and B, cast on 33 sts.

Beg with a RS (k) row, work 20 rows in st-st stripe sequence as foll:

4 rows B, 4 rows C, 4 rows D, 4 rows E and 4 rows A.

Rep last 20 rows 13 times more.

Cont in st-st, work 4 rows in B.

Change to long 3¼mm(US 3) circular needle and C.

Next row (RS) K33, pick up and k 284 sts along one edge of scarf (1 st in each row), 33 sts across cast-on edge and 284 sts along rem edge of scarf. 634 sts.

Working in rounds, p 1 round, k 1 round, then cast/bind off purlwise on next round.

cabled hat with earflaps

Children will love this hat with its bunny-tail bobble on top. The ties will keep it firmly in place and the earflaps will make sure that little ears stay snug and warm.

materials

One 50g/1¾oz ball each of King Cole *Anti-Tickle Merino DK* in main colour **M** (turquoise/Turquoise 18; or hot pink/Raspberry 67) and contrasting colour **A** (blue/Bluebell 26; or cream/Aran 46)

Cable needle

Pair of 3¾mm(US 5) knitting needles 3¼mm(US 3) circular needle

sizes

small   medium   large

tension/gauge

23 sts and 32 rows to 10cm/4in over st-st using 3¾mm(US 5) needles

abbreviations

beg beginning; **cm** centimetre(s); **C6F (cable 6 front)** sl next 3 sts onto cable needle and hold at front, k3, then k3 from cable needle; **in** inch(es); **k** knit; **kfb** k into front and back of next st to inc 1 st; **p** purl; **patt** pattern; **pfb** p into front and back of next st to inc 1 st; **rem** remaining; **RS** right side; **sl** slip; **skpo** sl 1, k1, pass slipped st over; **sk2togpo** sl 1, k2tog, pass slipped st over; **st(s)** stitch(es); **st-st** stocking/stockinette stitch; **tog** together; **WS** wrong side

earflaps (make 2)

With 3¾mm(US 5) needles and M, cast on 10 sts.

1st row (RS) Kfb, p1, k6, p1, kfb. 12 sts.

2nd row Pfb, p1, k1, p6, k1, p1, pfb. 14 sts.

3rd row K3, p1, k6, p1, k3.

4th row Pfb, p2, k1, p6, k1, p2, pfb. 16 sts.

5th row (cable crossing row) Kfb, k3, p1, C6F, p1, k3, kfb. 18 sts.

6th row P5, k1, p6, k1, p5.

7th row K5, p1, k6, p1, k5.

8th and 9th rows As 6th and 7th rows.

10th row As 6th row.

11th row (cable crossing row) As 5th row.

12th–15th rows Rep 6th and 7th rows twice.

These last 15 rows set the position of the cable which is crossed on every foll 6th row.

Leave sts on a holder.

main hat

With WS of earflaps facing, 3¾mm(US 5) needles and M, cast on 14(16:18) sts, work [p5, k1, p6, k1, p5] across one earflap, cast on 42(50:58) sts, work [p5, k1, p6, k1, p5] across rem earflap, cast on 14(16:18) sts. 106(118:130) sts.

Foundation row (RS) K4, p1, k6, p1, k7(9:11), p1, C6F, p1, [k7(9:11), p1, k6, p1] 3 times, k7(9:11), p1, C6F, p1, k7(9:11), p1, k6, p1, k4.

1st row P4, [k1, p6, k1, p7(9:11)] 6 times, k1, p6, k1, p4.

2nd row K4, [p1, k6, p1, k7(9:11)] 6 times, p1, k6, p1, k4.

3rd and 4th rows As first and 2nd rows.

5th row As first row.

6th row K4, [p1, C6F, p1, k7(9:11)] 6 times, p1, C6F, p1, k4.

These last 6 rows form the patt and are repeated.

Cont in patt until work measures 7.5cm/3in from cast-on edge, ending with a 5th row.

3rd size only

Next row (RS) K4, [p1, C6F, p1, skpo, k7, k2tog] 6 times, p1, C6F, p1, k4. 118 sts.

Patt 5 rows.

2nd and 3rd sizes only

Next row (RS) K4, [p1, C6F, p1, skpo, k5, k2tog] 6 times, p1, C6F, p1, k4. 106 sts.

Patt 5 rows.

all sizes

Next row (RS) K2, [k2tog, p1, C6F, p1, skpo, k3] 6 times, k2tog, p1, C6F, p1, skpo, k2. 92 sts.

Patt 3 rows.

Next row (RS) K1, [k2tog, p1, k6, p1, skpo, k1] 6 times, k2tog, p1, k6, p1, skpo, k1. 78 sts.

Patt 3 rows.

Next row (RS) K2, [p1, k6, p1, sk2togpo] 6 times, p1, k6, p1, k2. 66 sts.

Patt 1 row.

Next row (RS) K1, p2tog, [k6, p3tog] 6 times, k6, p2tog, k1. 52 sts.

Patt 1 row.

Next row (RS) K1, [p1, C6F] 7 times, p1, k1.

Next row P1, p2tog, [p1, p2tog, p1, p3tog] 6 times, [p1, p2tog] twice, p1. 31 sts.

Next row [K2tog, k2] 7 times, k2tog, k1. 23 sts.

Next row [P1, p2tog] 7 times, p2. 16 sts.

Next row K1, [k2tog] 7 times, k1. 9 sts.

Next row [P3tog] 3 times.

Break yarn leaving a 30cm/12in length for sewing up, thread through rem 3 sts, pull up and secure.

edging

With RS facing, 3¼mm(US 3) circular needle and A, pick up and k 13(15:17) sts across cast-on sts, 37 sts around right earflap, 42(50:58) sts across front cast-on sts, 37 sts around left earflap, and 13(15:17) sts across cast-on sts. 142(154:166) sts.

K 2 rows.

Cast/bind off knitwise.

to finish

Join back seam. Make a pompon from A and stitch to the top of the hat.

bold banded mittens

Mittens on strings are a great idea. Simply thread these striped mittens through your child's winter coat and the string will stop them from losing one.

materials

One 50g/1¾oz ball each of King Cole *Anti-Tickle Merino DK* in main colour **M** (red/Cherry 29 or cream/Aran 46) and **A** (cream/Aran 46; or blue/Bluebell 26)
Pair each of 3¼mm(US 3) and 3¾mm(US 5) knitting needles

sizes

to fit

3–6 mths	1–2	3–4	yrs

tension/gauge

23 sts and 32 rows to 10cm/4in over st-st using 3¾mm(US 5) needles

abbreviations

alt alternate; **beg** beginning; **cm** centimetre(s); **cont** continu(e)(ing); **dec** decrease; **foll** follow(s)(ing); **in** inch(es); **inc** increas(e)(ing); **k** knit; **m1** make one stitch by picking up and working into back of loop lying between last st and next st; **p** purl; **patt** pattern; **rem** remaining; **rep** repeat; **RS** right side; **ssk** sl 1 knitwise, sl 1 knitwise, insert tip of left needle into fronts of 2 slipped sts and k2tog through back of loops; **tog** together; **WS** wrong side

note

Mittens for smallest size have no thumbs and are identical.

right mitten

With 3¼mm(US 3) needles and M, cast on 27(31:35) sts.

1st rib row (RS) K1, [p1, k1] to end.
2nd rib row P1, [k1, p1] to end.

These last 2 rows form rib patt and are repeated.
Work 3(3:4)cm/1¼(1¼:1½)in in rib, ending with a 2nd rib row and inc 1 st in centre of last row for 3rd size only. 27(31:36) sts.
Change to 3¾mm(US 5) needles and A.

1st size only
Beg with a RS (k) row and working in 4-row st-st stripe repeat of 2 rows A, 2 rows M, work 12 rows.

2nd and 3rd sizes only
Beg with a RS (k) row and working in 4-row st-st stripe repeat of 2 rows A, 2 rows M, work (0:2) rows.**

shape for thumb
Keeping st-st stripe patt (2 rows A, 2 rows M) correct, shape thumb as foll:

Inc row (RS) K(16:18), m1, k(1:2), m1, k(14:16).
P 1 row.
Inc row (RS) K(16:18), m1, k(3:4), m1, k(14:16).
P 1 row.
Inc row (RS) K(16:18), m1, k(5:6), m1, k(14:16).
P 1 row.
Cont in this way, inc 2 st as set on every alt row until there are (41:46) sts, ending with a WS (p) row.
Next row (RS) K(27:30), turn.
***Work in (M:A) only as foll:
Next row Cast on 1 st, p(12:13) including cast-on st, turn and cast on 1 st.
Work 8 rows in st-st on these (13:14) sts only.
Next row [K2tog] 3 times, k(1:0), [k2tog] (3:4) times. 7 sts.
Break yarn, thread through 7 rem sts, pull up and secure. Join thumb seam.
With RS facing and keeping stripe patt correct, rejoin yarn to base of thumb, pick up and k (3:4) sts at base of thumb, then k rem sts. (33:38) sts.
Work 9 rows in stripe patt.

all sizes
Keeping stripe patt correct, shape top as foll:
Dec row K1, ssk, k8(11:13), k2tog, k1(1:2), ssk, k8(11:13), k2tog, k1.
Work 3 rows.

Dec row K1, ssk, k6(9:11), k2tog, k1(1:2), ssk, k6(9:11), k2tog, k1.
Work 1(1:3) rows.
Dec row K1, ssk, k4(7:9), k2tog, k1(1:2), ssk, k4(7:9), k2tog, k1.
P 1 row.
Cast/bind off.

left mitten

1st size only
Work Left Mitten as for Right Mitten.
2nd and 3rd sizes only
Work as for Right Mitten to **.
shape for thumb
Keeping stripe patt (2 rows A, 2 rows M) correct, shape thumb as foll:
Inc row (RS) K(14:16), m1, k(1:2), m1, k(16:18)
P 1 row.
Inc row (RS) K(14:16), m1, k(3:4), m1, k(16:18).
P 1 row.
Inc row (RS) K(14:16), m1, k(5:6), m1, k(16:18).
P 1 row.
Cont in this way, inc 2 st as set on every alt row until there are (41:46) sts, ending with a WS (p) row.
Next row (RS) K(25:28), turn.
Complete as given for Right Mitten from *** to end.

to finish

Join seam. Make a 70(85:100)cm/27½(33½:39¼)in plait/braid as foll:
Cut three 2(2.5:3)m/2(2½:3)yd lengths of A, fold each length in half and tie the lengths together at folded end. Plait/braid the three doubled lengths into a single plait/braid and knot the end to secure. Stitch one end of the plait/braid to the seam inside the right mitten and the other end to the seam inside the left mitten. Thread the plait/braid through the sleeves of the child's coat, so one mitten hangs out of each sleeve end ready to wear.

polka dot bootees & hat

Knitted in luxuriously soft yarn, this hat and bootee set will make a stylish gift for a new baby.

materials

Bootees

One 50g/1¾oz ball each (see *Note*) of Debbie Bliss *Baby Cashmerino* in **A** (pale blue/Pale Blue 202; or beige/Stone 102; or pale pink/Pale Pink 600) and **B** (off-white/Ecru 101)

Pair of 3mm (US 2–3) knitting needles

Hat

One 50g/1¾oz ball each (see *Note*) of Debbie Bliss *Baby Cashmerino* in **A** (pale blue/Pale Blue 202; or beige/Stone 102; or pale pink/Pale Pink 600) and **B** (off-white/Ecru 101)

Pair of 3mm(US 2–3) knitting needles

sizes

Bootees

to fit

3–6 mths

Hat

to fit

3–6 mths 6–12 mths

tension/gauge

30 sts and 36 rows to 10cm/4in over patterned st-st using 3mm (US 2–3) needles

abbreviations

alt alternate; **cm** centimetre(s); **cont** continu(e)(ing); **dec** decrease; **in** inch(es); **foll** follow(s)(ing); **in** inch(es); **k** knit; **kfb** k into front and back of next st; **kp** knit then purl into next st; **m1** make one st by picking up and working into back of loop between last st and next st; **p** purl; **pfb** p into front and back of next st; **pk** purl then knit into next st; **rem** remaining; **rep** repeat; **RS** right side; **st(s)** stitch(es); **st-st** stocking/stockinette stitch; **tog** together; **WS** wrong side

note

Hat and bootees together can be made from one ball each in A and B.

to make bootees (makes 2)

Bootees are worked throughout on 3mm(US 2–3) needles and are worked in one piece starting at heel end of sole.

sole

With 3mm(US 2–3) needles and A, cast on 3 sts.

1st row (RS) K1, p1, k1.
2nd row Pk, pk, p1.
3rd row Kp, k1, p1, kp, k1. 7 sts.

hat chart

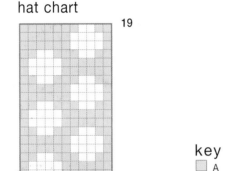

19

1

key

■ A
□ B

10 stitch repeat

edge stitch

bootee chart

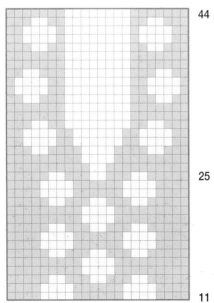

44

25

11

4th row [K1, p1] 3 times, k1.
5th row Pk, [p1, k1] twice, pk, p1.
6th row Kp, [k1, p1] 3 times, kp, k1.
7th row [K1, p1] 5 times, k1.
8th row Pk, [p1, k1] 4 times, pk, p1. 13 sts.
9th–36th rows [P1, k1] to last st, p1.
Dec 1 st at each end of next and 3 foll alt rows. 5 sts.
Next row (WS) P2, pfb, p2. 6 sts.

upper

Beg with a RS (k) row, work in st-st as foll:

1st row (RS) With A, kfb, k3, kfb, k1.
2nd row P in A.
3rd row With A, [kfb] twice, k3, [kfb] twice, k1. 12 sts.
4th row P in A.
5th row With A, [kfb] twice, k7, [kfb] twice, k1. 16 sts.
6th row P in A.
7th row KfbA, k6A, k2B, k5A, kfbA, k1A. 18 sts.
8th row P7A, p4B, p7A.
9th row K7A, k4B, k7A.
10th row [PfbA] twice, p1A, p2B, p3A, p2B, p3A, p2B, p2A, [pfbA] twice, p1A. 22 sts.
11th–24th rows Work in patterned st-st from bootee chart.
25th row Cont to work from chart, k5A, k2B, k3A, turn and cont on these sts only, leaving rem sts on a spare needle.
26th–44th rows Cont in st-st from chart **and at the same time** dec 1 st at ankle edge on 3 foll alt rows as indicated.
Cast/bind off.
With RS facing, slip 2 sts at centre front onto a safety pin, rejoin yarn to rem sts and complete chart.

cuff

With RS facing, 3mm(US 2–3) needles and A, pick up and k 19 sts down ankle edge to centre front, [k1, m1, k1] from sts on safety pin, then pick up and k 19 sts up ankle edge. 41 sts.

1st rib row (WS) P1, [k1, p1] to end.
2nd rib row (RS) K1, [p1, k1] to end.
Rep last 2 rows 12 more times.
Change to B.
Next row (WS) K.
Cast/bind off.

to make hat

With 3mm(US 2–3) needles and B, cast on 111 (121) sts.

Change to A and k 1 row.

1st rib row K1, [p1, k1] to end.

2nd rib row P1, [k1, p1] to end.

Rep last 2 rows until cuff measures 6.5(8)cm/2½(3¼)in from cast-on edge, ending with a 2nd rib row and dec 1 st in centre for 1st size only. 110(121) sts.

Beg with a RS (k) row work 2 rows. Now work 19 rows in st-st from hat chart and inc 1 st at end of last row for 1st size only. Cont in A only.

22nd row (WS) P1, [p2tog, p8] 11(12) times. 100 (109) sts.

Cont in st-st in A only, work 2 rows.

Next row (RS) [K7, k2tog] 11(12) times, k1. 89(97) sts.

Work 3 rows.

Next row [K6, k2tog] 11(12) times, k1. 78(85) sts. Work 3 rows.

Next row [K5, k2tog] 11(12) times, k1. 67(73) sts. Work 1(3) rows.

Next row [K4, k2tog] 11(12) times, k1. 56(61) sts. Work 1(3) rows.

Cont to dec 11(12) sts as set on every foll RS row until 23(25) sts rem. P 1 row.

Next row [K2tog] 11(12) times, k1. 12(13) sts.

Next row P0(1), [p2tog] 6 times. 6(7) sts.

Break yarn leaving a long end for sewing seam, thread through rem 6(7) sts, pull up and secure.

to finish

Join back seam, reversing lower part of ribbed cuff seam to allow for turn back. Make a pompon using B and sew to top of hat.

baby slippers

Who could resist these tiny shoes? They are easy to make and finished with simple cross stitch embroidery and stylish mother-of-pearl buttons.

materials

One 50g/1¾oz ball of Rowan *Cotton Glacé* in main colour **M** (red/Poppy 741) and small amount in **A** (off-white/Ecru 725)
Pair of 2¾mm(US 2) knitting needles
2 small buttons

sizes

to fit

| 3–6 | 6–12 | mths |

tension/gauge

28 sts and 44 rows to 10cm/4in over moss/seed st using 2¾mm (US 2) needles

abbreviations

alt alternate; **cm** centimetre(s); **cont** continu(e)(ing); **dec** decrease; **foll** follow(s)(ing); **in** inch(es); **inc** increase; **k** knit; **p** purl; **st(s)** stitch(es); **tog** together

note

Moss/seed st is reversible, so take care when you sew together the second slipper that it is a mirror image of the first.

slippers (makes 2)

Each slipper is made in one piece.

Sole

With 2¾mm(US 2) needles and M, cast on 20(24) sts.
Beg moss/seed st sole as foll:

1st row [K1, p1] to end.
2nd row Cast on 1 st, [p1, k1] to end, cast on 1 st.
22(26) sts.
3rd row [P1, k1] to end.
Cont in moss/seed st as set and taking inc sts into
moss/seed st, inc 1 st at each end of next and 2 foll alt
rows. 28(32) sts.
Keeping moss/seed st correct as set throughout, work 3
rows.
Dec 1 st at each end of next and 3 foll alt rows. 20(24) sts.
19th row Moss/seed st to end, cast on 7(8) sts. 27(32) sts

Upper

1st row Work in moss/seed st.
Inc 1 st at beg of next and every foll alt row until there
are 32(38) sts.
11th(13th) row Cast/bind off 12 sts, moss/seed st 5,
cast/bind off 4(5) sts, moss/seed st to end.
12th(14th) row Moss/seed st 11(16), leave 5 sts on a
safety pin for strap.
13th(15th)–21st(25th) rows Work in moss/seed st.

22nd(26th) row Moss/seed st 11(16), cast on
21(22) sts.
23rd(27th) row Work in moss/seed st.
Dec 1 st at beg of next and 4(5) foll alt rows.
Cast/bind off rem 27(32) sts.

strap

Slip 5 sts from safety pin onto a needle.
With 2¾mm(US 2) needles, work 21 rows in
moss/seed st as set.
Buttonhole row Moss/seed st 2, make *yarn-over* for
buttonhole by wrapping yarn around right needle,
work 2tog, moss/seed st 1.
Work 1 row in moss/seed st.
Next row Work 2tog, moss/seed st 1, work 2tog.
Cast/bind off rem 3 sts.

to finish

Join heel seam. Carefully stitch upper to sole, easing
in fullness at toe. Sew one button to each slipper.
Work cross stitches around edge in A.

snowflake hat & scarf

This hat and scarf looks great in a variety of colourways –
so why not make one to match your child's coat? Perfect
for days in the snow or just out and about with mummy.

materials

2 50g/1¾oz balls of Jaeger
  Matchmaker Merino DK in main
  colour **M** (red/Cherry 656) or
  (blue/Pacific) and 2 balls in **A**
  (cream/Cream 662)
Pair each of 3¾mm(US 5) and
  4mm(US 6) knitting needles
Spare knitting needles

sizes

to fit

1	2	3
6mths–1yr	1–2	2–3yrs

tension/gauge

22 sts and 30 rows to 10cm/4in
over st-st using 4mm(US 6) needles

abbreviations

cm centimetre(s); **cont** continue;
foll(s) follow(s)(ing); **inc**
increas(e)(ing); **in** inch(es); **k** knit;
k2tog knit next 2 sts together; **mm**
millimetre(s); **p** purl; **p2tog** purl
next 2 sts together; **rem**
remain(ing); **rep** repeat; **RS** right
side; **st(s)** stitch(es); **st-st**
stocking/stockinette stitch

note

When working from chart, use separate small
balls of yarn for each colour area and twist
yarns at colour change to avoid holes.

hat

With 4mm(US 6) needles and M, cast on 7 (9:11) sts.
Work in st-st beg with a k row and 2-row stripes as folls:

1st row With M, k, inc 1 st at each end of row. 9(11:13) sts.

2nd row With M, p, inc 1 st at each end of row. 11(13:15) sts.

3rd row With A, k.

4th row With A, p, inc 1 st at each end of row. 13(15:17) sts.

5th row With M, k,inc 1 st at each end of row. 15(17:19) sts.

6th row With M,p.

7th row With A, k, inc 1 st at each end of row. 17(19:21) sts.

8th row With A, p.

9th–14th (16th:18th) rows Work in st-st without shaping keeping stripe pattern correct.

Leave sts on spare needle.

Make second earflap to match.

With 3¾mm(US 5) needles and M, cast on 12(13:17) sts, k across 17(19:21) sts of first ear flap, cast on 32(36:44) sts, k across 17(19:21) sts of second ear flap, cast on 12(13:17) sts. 90(100:120) sts.

Work 3 rows in st-st, starting with a p row.

Change to 4mm(US 6) needles and work snowflake motif as folls:

1st row K38(43:53), work 14 sts from 1st row of snowflake chart, k38(43:53).

2nd row P38(43:53), work 14 sts from 2nd row of snowflake chart, p38(43:53).

3rd–16th rows Complete all 16 rows of chart.

Work a further 2(4:6) rows in st-st in M.

shape top (all sizes)

1st row K.

2nd row *P2tog, p8, rep from * to end. 81(90:108) sts.

3rd row K.

4th row P.

5th row *K7, k2tog, rep from * to end. 72(80:96) sts.

6th row P.

7th row K.

8th row *P2tog, p6, rep from * to end. 63(70:84) sts.

9th row K.

10th row P.

11th row *K5, k2tog, rep from * to end. 54 (60:72) sts.

size 1

12th row *P4, p2tog, rep from * to end. 45 sts.

13th row *K3, k2tog rep from * to end. 36 sts.

14th row *P2tog rep from * to end. 18 sts.

15th row *K2tog, rep from * to end. 9 sts.

size 2

12th row P.

13th row *K4, k2tog, rep from * to end. 50 sts.

14th row P.

15th row *K3, k2tog, rep from * to end. 40 sts.
16th row *P2tog, rep from * to end. 20 sts.
17th row *K2tog, rep from * to end. 10 sts.
size 3
12th row P.
13th row *K4, k2tog, rep from * to end. 60 sts.
14th row P.
15th row *K3, k2tog, rep from * to end. 48 sts.
16th row P.
17th row *K2, k2tog, rep from * to end. 36 sts.
18th row *P2tog, p1, rep from * to end. 24 sts.
19th row *K2tog, rep from * to end. 12 sts.
all sizes
Thread yarn through rem sts, draw up tightly and
fasten off securely

edging

With RS facing, 3¾mm(US 5) needles and M, pick up
and k 12(14:17) sts from back cast-on edge, 31(37:43)
sts around ear flap, 32(36:44) sts from front cast-on
edge, 31(37:43) sts around ear flap and 12(14:17) sts
from back cast-on edge. 118(136:164) sts.
Cast/bind off knitwise.

to finish

Join back seam. Weave in loose ends. Cut three
60cm/24in lengths of M. Thread half the length
through bottom centre of ear flap. Taking one end from
front and one end from back, make a plait with two
ends per strand. Knot at end and trim. Rep for second
earflap.

scarf

With 4mm(US 6) needles and M, cast on 32 sts.
Work 4 rows in st-st.
5th row (place motif) K9, work 1st row of chart, k9.
Cont to completion of chart. Work 4 more rows.
Change to stripes of *2 rows A, 2 rows M* until scarf
measures 120cm/46in, ending with 2 rows A.
Work 4 more rows in M then work chart again, but
this time turn it upside down and work 16th–1st rows
in intarsia.

Work 4 rows in M.
Cast/bind off.

edgings

With 3¾mm(US 5) needles and A, pick up and k 32 sts at
end of scarf.
Cast/bind off knitwise.
Repeat for other end.
With 33/4mm(US 5) needles and A, pick up and k 276 sts
along scarf.
Cast/bind off knitwise.
Repeat for other side.

finishing

Weave in loose ends. Neaten scarf corners.

snowflake motif

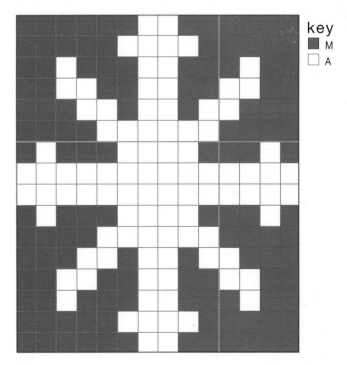

key
■ M
□ A

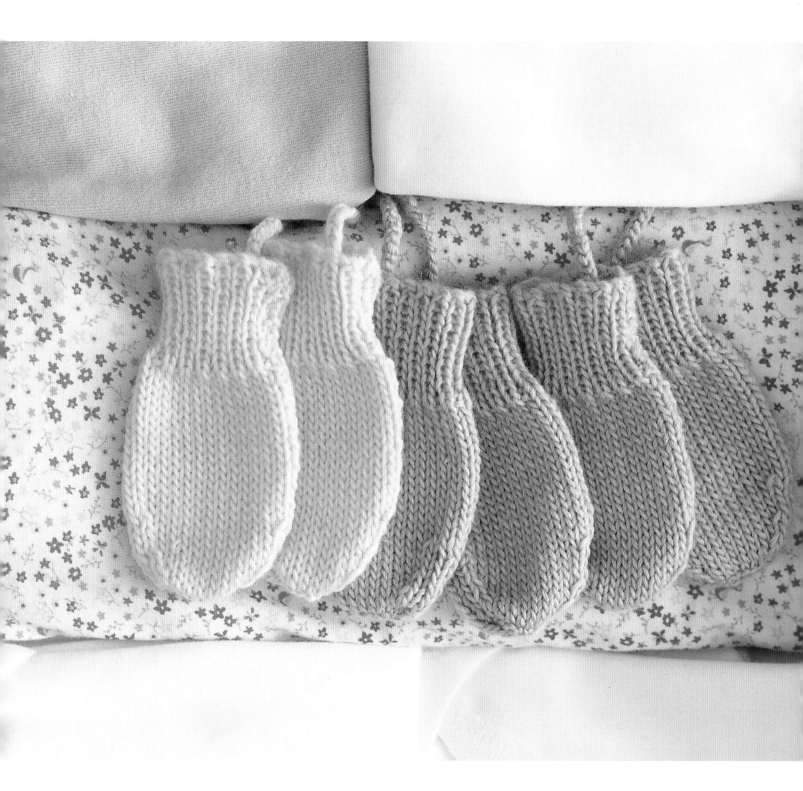

mini mittens

These cashmere mittens are so soft and cosy – perfect tiny warmers for perfect newborn hands. They are quick and easy to knit in an evening and make luxurious gifts.

materials

1 50g/1¾oz ball of Jaeger *Cashmina* in either (pale pink/Tea Rose 040), (pale green/Verdigris 042) or (pale blue/Sky 043)

Pair each of 3mm(US 2–3) and 3¼mm(US 3) knitting needles

size

to fit

0–3 mths

tension/gauge

28 sts and 38 rows to 10cm/4in over st-st using 3¼mm(US 3) needles

abbreviations

beg begin(ning); **cm** centimetre(s); **in** inch(es); **k** knit; **k2tog** knit next 2 sts together; **mm** millimetre(s); **p** purl; **rem** remain(ing); **rep** repeat; **RS** right side; **skpo** sl1, k1, psso; **s1** slip next stitch; **st(s)** stitch(es); **st-st** stocking/stockinette stitch; **WS** wrong side

to make (make 2)

With 3mm(US 2–3) needles, cast on 31 sts.

1st row (RS) K1, *p1, k1, rep from * to end.

2nd row (WS) P1, *k1, p1 from * to end.

Rep these 2 rows for 3cm/1¼in, ending with a 2nd row.

Change to 3¼mm(US 3) needles and beg with a k row, work 16 rows in st-st.

shape top

Next row (RS) K1, skpo, k10, k2tog, k1, skpo, k10, k2tog, k1. 27 sts.

Work 3 rows in st-st without shaping.

Next row (RS) K1, skpo, k8, k2tog, k1, skpo, k8, k2tog, k1. 23 sts.

Next row P.

Next row K1, skpo, k6, k2tog, k1, skpo, k6, k2tog, k1. 19 sts.

Next row P.

Cast/bind off.

to finish

Join seam.

Make a 71cm/28in plaited braid and sew one end to inside of each mitten on seam.

cashmere bootees

These little bootees make a great gift for precious new arrivals. Lovely in any colour combination, they feel gloriously luxurious in soft cashmere yarn.

materials

1 50g/1¾oz ball of Jaeger *Cashmina* in each of main colour **M** (dark pink/Cyclamen 047) and **A** (pale pink/Tea Rose 040) or **M** (grey/Pewter 045) and **A** (ecru/Ecru 030)

Pair of 3mm(US 2–3) knitting needles

size

to fit

6–9mths

tension/gauge

28 sts and 38 rows to 10cm/4in over st-st using 3mm(US 2–3) needles

abbreviations

cm centimetre(s); **foll(s)** follow(s)(ing); **g-st (garter stitch)** every row knit; **in** inch(es); **k** knit; **k2tog** knit next 2 sts together; **mm** millimetre(s); **p** purl; **patt** pattern; **rep** repeat; **RS** right side; **st(s)** stitch(es); **st-st** stocking/stockinette stitch; **yo (yarn over needle)** take yarn over right needle to make a st

to make (make 2)

With 3mm(US 2–3) needles and M cast on 41 sts and work 2cm/¾in in g-st.

Change to st-st and work 4 rows.

5th row K2*yo, k2tog,k2, rep from * 8 times, yo, k2tog, k1.

6th row P.

divide for top of foot

7th row K28, turn, p15, turn.

On 15 sts, work stripe patt as folls:

1st row (RS) K in A.

2nd row P in A.

3rd row K in M.

4th row P in M.

5th–20th rows Rep 1st–4th rows 4 times.

21st–22nd rows Rep 1st and 2nd rows once (toe). Break yarns. With RS facing (13 sts on right needle), rejoin M and pick up and k 16 sts along side of foot, k 15 sts from toe, k 16 sts along side of foot and k 13 sts on left needle. 73 sts.

Work 13 rows in g-st.

shape sole

1st row K1, *k2tog, k30, k2tog* k3, then rep * to * again, k1. 69 sts.

2nd row K31, k2tog, k3, k2tog, k31. 67 sts.

3rd row K1, *k2tog, k27, k2tog* k3, then rep * to * again, k1. 63 sts.

4th row K28, k2tog, k3, k2tog, k28. 61 sts.

5th row K1, *k2tog, k24, k2tog* k3, then rep * to * again, k1. 57 sts.

Cast/bind off.

to finish

Join leg seam and under foot seam. Weave in any loose ends and plait 3 lengths of A together to make ties 43cm/17in long, knotting ends to secure them. Thread ties through eyelets and tie in a bow.

nursery comforts

my first teddy

This woolly bear with his stripy scarf and smiley face is just the sort of bear to become a treasured heirloom. Why not knit a few and have your own teddy bears' picnic?

materials

Teddy: 2 50g/1¾oz balls of Rowan *Cork* in main colour **M** (brown/ Mouse 042)

Scarf: 1 50g/1¾oz ball of Rowan 4 ply *Soft* in each of **A** (red/Honk 374) and **B** (ecru/Nippy 376)

Pair each of 3mm(US 2–3) and 4½mm(US 7) knitting needles

2 safety pins

Washable stuffing

Black or brown yarn for eyes and nose embroidery

size

41cm/16in tall

tension/gauge

Teddy: 12 sts and 18 rows to 10cm/ 4in over st-st using 4½mm(US 7) needles

Scarf: 28 sts and 36 rows to 10cm/ 4in over st-st using 3mm(US 2–3) needles

abbreviations

alt alternate; **cm** centimetre(s); **cont** continue; **dec** decreas(e)(ing); **foll(s)** follow(s)(ing); **inc** increas(e)(ing); **in** inch(es); **inc** increase in next stitch; **k** knit; **k2tog** knit next 2 sts together; **m1** make 1 st by picking up and working into back of loop lying between last st and next st; **mm** millimetre(s); **p** purl; **p2tog** purl next 2 sts together; **patt** pattern; **psso** pass slipped st over; **rem** remain(ing); **rep** repeat; **RS** right side; **s1** slip next st; **skpo** s1, k1, psso; **st(s)** stitch(es); **st-st** stocking/stockinette stitch; **tbl** through back of loop; **WS** wrong side

1st row K7, cast/bind off 10 sts, k14, cast/bind off 10 sts, k3, place last 4 sts on safety pin.

work head

WS facing, p3, p14, p3, place last 4 sts on safety pin. 20 sts on needle.

shape face

1st row K10, m1, k10. 21 sts.
2nd row Inc in 1st st, p to last 2 sts, inc in next st, p1. 23 sts.
3rd row K11, m1, k1, m1, k11. 25 sts.
4th row As 2nd row. 26 sts.
5th row K13, m1, k1, m1, k13. 29 sts.
6th row As 2nd row. 31 sts.
7th row K15, m1, k1, m1, k15. 33 sts.
8th row As 2nd row. 35 sts.
9th row K17, m1, k1, m1, k17. 37 sts.
10th row As 2nd row. 39 sts.
11th row K19, m1, k1, m1, k19. 41 sts.
Work 2 rows in st-st.
14th row P20, cast/bind off 1 st, p20.
15th row On 20 sts, k18, k2tog. 19 sts.
16th row P2tog, p17. 18 sts.
17th row K16, k2tog. 17 sts.
18th row P.
19th row Skpo, k13, k2tog. 15 sts.
20th row P.
21st row Skpo, k11, k2tog. 13 sts.
22nd row P2tog, p9, p2tog. 11 sts.
23rd row Cast/bind off 3 sts, k to end. 8 sts.
24th row Cast/bind off 3 sts, p to end. 5 sts.
Cast/bind off.
With RS facing rejoin yarn to rem 20 sts and work from 15th row to end, reversing all shapings.

shape top of head

Sew small shoulder seams and centre back body seam. Place sts on safety pins back onto needle. 8 sts.
With RS facing, rejoin yarn and work as follows:
1st row K.
2nd row Inc in 1st st, p to last 2 sts, inc in next st, p1. 10 sts.
3rd–10th rows Rep 1st–2nd rows 4 times. 18 sts.
11th–20th rows Work in st-st without shaping.
21st row K2tog, k to last 2 sts, skpo. 16 sts.
22nd–30th rows Work in st-st without shaping.

body

With 4½mm(US 7) needles and M, cast on 40 sts.
1st row *K2, inc in next st, k2, rep from * to end. 48 sts.
Starting with a p row, cont in st-st until work measures 12.5cm/5in, ending with a p row.

31st row K2tog, k to last 2 sts, skpo. 14 sts.
32nd–36th rows Work in st-st without shaping.
37th row K2tog, k to last 2 sts, skpo. 12 sts.
38th row P.
39th row K2tog, k to last 2 sts, skpo. 10 sts.
40th row P.
41st and 43rd rows K2tog, k to last 2 sts, skpo.
42nd and 44th rows P2tog tbl, k to last 2 sts, skpo.
2 sts.
45th row K2tog. Fasten off.
Carefully ease top of head piece around face and sew.
Stuff head and body. Sew lower body seam.

legs
With 4½mm(US 7) needles and M, cast on 12 sts.
1st row *K1, inc in next st, rep from * to end. 18 sts.
2nd row P.
3rd row Inc in 1st st, k6, inc in next st, k2, inc in
next st, k6, inc in next st. 22 sts.
4th row P.
5th row K8, inc in next st, k3, inc in next st, k9. 24
sts
6th–10th rows Work in st-st without shaping.
11th row K10, skpo, k2tog, k10. 22 sts.
12th row P.
13th row K9, skpo, k2tog, k9. 20 sts.
Work 31 rows in st-st without shaping.
Cast/bind off.
Make second leg to match.
RS facing, join foot and leg seam, leaving cast/bind-off
edge open. Turn RS out and stuff. Make seam centre
back of leg and close opening. Attach legs to body.

arms
left arm
With 4½mm(US 7) needles and M, cast on 16 sts.
1st row *Inc in 1st st, k6 [inc in next st] twice, k6, inc
in next st. 20 sts.
Work 23 rows in st-st, starting with a p row. #
work paw
25th row K3, p1, k1, p1, k14.
26th row P13, *k1, p1, rep from * once, k1, p2.
27th–32nd row Rep 25th–26th rows 3 times.

33rd row As 25th row.
34th row *P2tog, p6, p2tog, rep from * once. 16 sts.
35th row K.
36th row *P1, p2tog, rep from * to last stitch, p1.
Cast/bind off.
right arm
Work as for Left Arm from # to #.
work paw
25th row K14, p1, k1, p1, k3.
26th row P2, *k1, p1, rep from * once, k1, p13.
Cont and finish as for Left Arm, noting paw position.
RS facing, join arm seam, leaving cast/bind-off edge
open. Turn RS out and stuff. Close opening. Attach to
body with seams on the underside of the arm.

ears (make 2)
With 4½mm(US 7) needles and M, cast on 10 sts.
Work 3 rows in st-st.
Dec 1 st at each end of next and foll alt row. 6 sts.
Work 1 row in st-st without shaping.
8th row *K1, p1, rep from * to end.
9th row Inc in 1st st, *k1 p1, rep from * once, inc in
next st. 8 sts.
10th–14th row Work in moss/seed st.
Cast/bind off in moss/seed st.
Make second ear to match.
Fold ear in half and sew side seams. Attach to head
with moss/seed st as front of ear.

to finish
Weave in loose ends. Embroider eyes, mouth and nose.

scarf
With 3mm(US 2–3) needles and A, cast on 15 sts.
Work approximately 50cm/20in in moss/seed st with
stripe patt of *4 rows A, 4 rows B*, ending with 4
rows A.
Cast/bind off.
Weave in loose ends. Tie scarf around Teddy's neck.

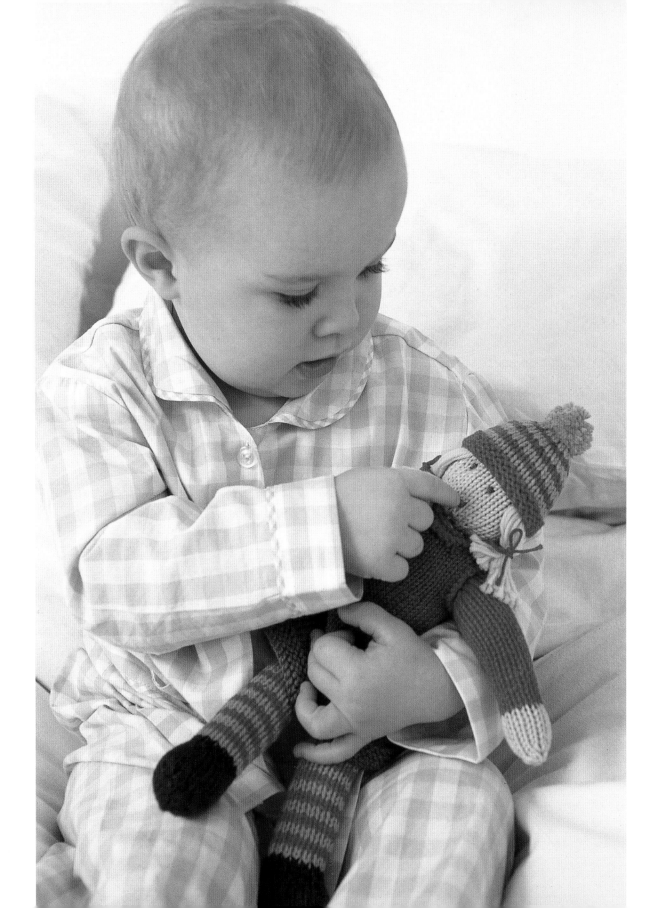

darling dolly

This dolly is a firm favourite with my little one and is a good way to use up oddments of yarn. Try knitting several different dollies, then they can all play together.

materials

Oddments of Jaeger *Aqua Cotton* in (orange/Marigold 331), (dark pink/India 322), (flesh colour/Talc 302), (yellow/Daffodil 330), (red/Ruby 316) and (purple/Comfrey328)

Pair of 3mm(US 2–3) knitting needles

Crochet hook

Washable stuffing

size

31cm/12⅛in tall

tension/gauge

26 sts and 36 rows to 10cm/4in over st-st using 3mm(US 2–3) needles

abbreviations

alt alternate; **beg** begin(ning); **cm** centimetre(s); **cont** continue; **in** inch(es); **inc** increase(e)(ing); **k** knit; **k2tog** knit next 2 sts together; **mm** millimetre(s); **p** purl; **p2tog** purl next 2 sts together; **patt** pattern; **psso** pass slipped st over; **rem** remain(ing); **rep** repeat; **RS** right side; **s1** slip next st; **skpo** s1, k1, psso; **st(s)** stitch(es); **st-st** stocking/stockinette stitch; **WS** wrong side

note

Work in st-st throughout unless specified otherwise.

body

With 3mm(US 2–3) needles and body colour, cast on 24 sts and work 2 rows in st-st marking the 12th and 13th sts.

3rd row *K2, inc in next st, rep from * to end. 32 sts.
Work 25 rows st-st without shaping beg with p row.

shape shoulders

1st row K6, skpo, k2tog, k12, skpo, k2tog, k6. 28 sts.
2nd and 4th rows P.
3rd row K5, skpo, k2tog, k10, skpo, k2tog, k5. 24 sts.
5th row K4, skpo, k2tog, k8, skpo, k2tog, k4. 20 sts.
6th row K.
7th row Change to flesh colour. Work 2 rows in st-st beg with a k row.

shape head

1st row *K1, inc in next st, rep from * to end. 30 sts.
Work 21 rows in st-st beg with a p row.

shape top of head

1st row *K3, k2tog*, rep from * to end. 24 sts.
2nd and 4th rows P.
3rd row *K3, k2tog, rep from * to end. 18 sts.
5th row *K1, k2tog, rep from * to end. 12 sts.
6th row *P2tog, rep from * to end. 6 sts.
Break yarn leaving 25cm/10in end. Thread yarn through remaining 6 stitches and pull up tightly. Fasten securely. Join head seam and body seam (row ends), leaving an opening for stuffing. Place seam between markers on cast-on edge and oversew across cast-on edge, making

the seam centre back. Turn RS out and stuff firmly. Close opening. Embroider eyes, nose and mouth.

legs (make 2)

With 3mm(US 2–3) needles and shoe colour, cast on 14 sts.

1st row *K1, inc in next st, rep from * to end. 21 sts.
2nd row P.
3rd row K7, *inc in next st, k1 rep from * 3 times, k6. 25 sts.
4th–10th rows Work in st-st without shaping, beg with a p row.
11th row K7, [skpo] twice, s1, k2tog, psso, [k2tog] twice, k7. 19 sts.
12th row P.
13th row K2tog, k15, k2tog. 17 sts.
Change to stocking colours and work 36 rows in st-st in 2-row stripes, starting with a p row.
49th row P1, p2tog, p3, p2tog, p1, p2tog, p3, p2tog, p1. 13 sts.
Cast/bind off.
Join stocking and shoe seams leaving cast/bind-off edge open. Turn RS out and stuff. Make stocking seam centre back of leg and close opening. Attach legs to body.

arms (make 2)

With 3mm(US 2–3) needles and flesh colour, cast on 4 sts.

1st row Inc in each stitch. 8 sts.
2nd row P.
3rd row Inc in 1st st, k2, [inc in next st] twice, k2, inc in next st.
4th row Inc in 1st st, p9, inc in next st, p1. 14 sts.
Work 6 rows in st-st without shaping, beg with a knit row.
Change to dark pink and work 25 rows in st-st, inc 1 st at each end of row 11. 16 sts.
Next row *P2, p2tog, rep from * to end. 12 sts.
Cast/bind off.
Join arm seam, leaving cast/bind-off edge open. Turn RS out and stuff. Close opening. Attach to body,

having the seams on the underside of the arm and the top of the arm at the second shoulder decrease.

dress

With 3 mm(US 2–3) needles and dress colour, cast on 60 sts and k5 rows.
Change to st-st and work 32 rows, beg with a k row, decreasing on rows 11, 21 and 31 rows as follows:
11th row K3, *skpo, k8, skpo, k2tog, k8, k2tog* k6, rep * to * once, k3. 52 sts.
21st row K3, *skpo, k6, skpo, k2tog, k6, k2tog*, k6, rep from * to * once, k3. 44 sts.
31st row K3, *skpo, k4, skpo, k2tog, k4, k2tog*, k6, rep from * to * once, k3. 36 sts.
shape armholes
33rd row K8, cast/bind off 2 sts, k16, cast/bind off 2 sts, k8.
On 8 sts, work Right Back.
1st row P6, p2tog. 7 sts.
2nd–8th rows Work in st-st.
shape neck
9th row Cast/bind off 3 sts, p to end. 4 sts.
10th row K.
11th row P2tog, p2. 3 sts.
12th row K.
13th row P.
Cast/bind off.
On 16 sts, work front.
1st row WS facing, rejoin yarn, p2tog, p12, p2tog. 14 sts.
Work 6 rows in st-st.
shape neck
8th row K5, cast/bind off 4 sts, k5.
**Dec 1 st at neck edge on next and foll alt row.
Work 2 rows.
Cast/bind off**.
Rejoin yarn to right front neck and work from ** to ** to match.
left back
WS facing, rejoin yarn to rem 8 sts and work to match Right Back.

edgings
arm trims (both alike)
With RS facing and with 3mm(US 2–3) needles and a contrast colour, pick up 24 sts around armhole.
Cast/bind off knitwise.
Join shoulder seams.
neck trim
With RS facing and with 3mm(US 2–3) needles and a contrasting colour, pick up 30 sts around neck.
Cast/bind off knitwise.

to finish
Join centre back seam from hem to armhole. **Do not break thread**. Fit dress onto doll and complete centre back seam.

hat
With 3mm(US 2–3) needles and one of the colours used for the stockings, cast on 32 sts and k 5 rows.
Change to other stocking colour and work 8 rows in 2-row stripes, starting with a knit row.
shape top
1st row *K2 k2tog, rep from * to end. 24 sts.
Work 3 rows st-st.
5th row *K1, k2tog, rep from * to end. 16 sts.
Work 3 rows st-st.
9th row *K2tog, rep from * to end. 8 sts.
10th row *P2tog, rep from * to end. 4 sts.
Finish off as for top of head. Sew side seam. Buy (or make) small pompon and attach to top of hat.

hair
Cut long strands of yarn, fold in half and knot through knitted stitches on head using a crochet hook. Part strands along centre of head to form two bunches and tie with lengths of contrasting yarn. Trim strands to neaten.

playful penguin

This fun penguin with its bright orange beak and feet is great for newborns as well as toddlers. Its monotone colour scheme is also said to stimulate babies.

materials

1 50g/1¾oz ball of Jaeger *Matchmaker Merino DK* in main colour **M** (black/Black 681) and small amounts in **A** (cream/Cream 622) and **B** (orange/Pumpkin 898).

Oddment of yellow yarn for eyes

Pair of 3mm(US 2–3) knitting needles

Washable stuffing

size

20cm/8in tall

tension/gauge

28 sts and 38 rows to 10cm/4in over st-st using 3mm(US 2–3) needles

abbreviations

beg begin(ning); **cm** centimetre(s); **cont** continue; **dec** decreas(e)(ing); **foll(s)** follow(s)(ing); **inc** increas(e)(ing); **in** inch(es); **k** knit; **k2tog** knit next 2 sts together; **mm** millimetre(s); **p** purl; **p2tog** purl next 2 sts together; **rem** remain(ing); **st(s)** stitch(es); **st-st** stocking/stockinette stitch; **tbl** through back of loops

base

With 3mm (US 2–3) needles and M, cast on 28 sts.
Work 19 rows in st-st, dec 1 st at each end of 5th, 9th,
13th, 17th and 19th rows. 18 sts.
Work 1 row.
Dec 1 st at each end of next 4 rows. 10 sts.
Cast/bind off 3 sts at beg next 2 rows. 4 sts.
Cast/bind off.

body

With 3mm (US 2–3) needles and M, cast on 79 sts.
Work 6 rows in st-st, inc 1 st at each end of 3rd and
6th rows. 83 sts.
7th row K39M, k5A, k39M.
8th row P37M, p9A, p37M.
9th row Inc in 1st st, k35M, k11A, k35M, inc in last
st. 85 sts.
10th row P36M, p13A, p36M.
11th row K36M, k13A, k36M.
12th row P35M, p15A, p35M.
13th row K2tog, k33M, k15A, k33M, k2tog tbl. 83
sts.
14th row P2tog tbl, p32M, p15A, p32M, p2tog, 81
sts.
15th row K2tog, k31M, k15A, k31M, k2tog tbl. 79
sts.
16th row P32M, p15A, p32M.
17th row K2tog, k30M, k15A, k30M, k2tog tbl. 77
sts.
18th row P31M, p15A, p31M.
19th row K31M, k15A, k31M.
20th row P2tog tbl, p21M, p2tog tbl, p6M, p15A,
p6M, p2tog, p21M, p2tog. 73 sts.
21st, 23rd, 25th and 27th rows K29M, k15A,
k29M.
22nd, 24th, 26th and 28th rows P29M, p15A,
p29M.
29th row K2tog, k20M, k2tog, k5M, k15A, k5M,
k2tog tbl, k20M, k2tog tbl. 69 sts.
30th row P27M, p15A, p27M.
31st row K27M, k15A, k27M.
32nd and 34th rows P28M, p13A, p28M.
33rd row K28M, k13A, k28M.
35th row K2tog. k19M, k2tog, k5M, k13A, k5M,

k2tog tbl, k19M, k2tog tbl. 65 sts.
36th row P26M, p13A, p26M.
37th row K26M, k13A, k26M.
38th row P27M, p11A, p27M.
39th row K27M, k11A, k27M.
40th row P28M, p9A, p28M.
41st row K7M, k2tog, k14M, k2tog, k5M, k5A, k5M, k2tog tbl, k14M, k2tog tbl, k7M. 61 sts.
Break A.
42nd–46th rows Work in st-st using M only.
Cont in st-st using M to 70th row, shaping as follows (shaping rows ONLY given from this point).
47th row K6, k2tog, k14, k2tog, k13, k2tog, k14, k2tog, k6. 57 sts.
53rd row K6, k2tog, k12, k2tog, k13, k2tog, k12, k2tog, k6. 53 sts.
59th row K5, k2tog, k12, k2tog, k11, k2tog, k12, k2tog, k6. 49 sts.
65th row *K4, k2tog, rep from * to last st, k1. 41 sts.
66th row P1, *p2tog, p3, rep from * to end. 33 sts.
67th row *K2tog, k2, rep from * to last st, k1. 25 sts.
68th row P1, *p2tog, p1, rep from * to end. 17 sts.
69th row *K2tog, rep from * to last st, k1. 9 sts.
70th row P1, *p2tog, rep from * to end. 5 sts.
Break yarn and thread through rem sts, draw tightly and fasten off securely.

wings (both alike)

With 3mm(US 2–3) needles and M, cast on 6 sts and knit 1 row.
Cont in st-st.
Cast on 2 sts beg of next 2 rows. 10 sts.
Work 1 row.
Inc 1 st at each end of next and foll 4th row. 14 sts.
Work 21 rows without shaping.
Dec 1 st at each end of next and foll 4th row. 10 sts.
Work 1 row.
Cast/bind off 2 sts beg next 2 rows. 6 sts.
Cast/bind off.

beak

With 3mm(US 2–3) needles and B, cast on 17 sts and knit 4 rows in st-st.

Cont in st-st, dec 1 st at each end of next 7 rows. 3 sts.
Work 1 row.
Inc 1 st at each end of next 7 rows. 17 sts.
Work 5 rows st-st without shaping.
Cast/bind off.

feet (both alike)

With 3mm(US 2–3) needles and B, cast on 13 sts and work 16 rows in st-st, inc 1 st at each end of 7th and 13th rows. 17 sts.
Cont in st-st to 32nd row, dec 1 st at each end of 21st and 27th rows. 13 sts.
Cast/bind off.

to finish

Fold beak in half widthways and sew side seams. Fold feet in half widthways and sew side seams. Embroider toes with M. Attach feet to cast-on edge of base. Join centre back seam of body from head to halfway down. Insert base with the cast-on edge and feet to front of body and cast/bind-off edge of base to tail side of body. Sew into position, then sew tail and back seam of body, leaving opening for stuffing. Stuff body and close opening. Stuff beak and sew in a rounded shape to face. Embroider eyes with yellow yarn. Fold wings in half lengthways and sew side seams. Attach to body.

zoo toy bag

Handy for trips to grandma's house, this elephant-design toy bag will hold lots of favourite toys. At home, it looks stylish hanging on the nursery door and keeps toys tidy.

materials

3 balls of Rowan *Handknit DK Cotton* in **A** (dark green/Slippery 316), 2 balls in **B** (pale green/Celery 309), 2 balls in **C** (yellow/Zing 300), 2 balls in **D** (ecru/Ecru 251), 2 balls in **E** (beige/Linen 205) and 2 balls in **F** (dark beige/Tope 253)
Pair of 4mm(US 6) knitting needles
Spare knitting needle

size

45 x 53cm/18 x 21in

tension/gauge

20 sts and 28 rows to 10cm/4in over st-st using 4mm(US 6) needles

abbreviations

cm centimetre(s); **foll(s)** follow(s)(ing); **in** inch(es); **k** knit; **mm** millimetre(s); **p** purl; **RS** right side; **st(s)** stitch(es); **st-st** stocking/stockinette stitch

note

Work in st-st throughout. When working from chart, use separate small balls of yarn for each colour area and twist yarns at colour change to avoid holes.

pocket lining

With 4mm(US 6) needles and E, cast on 36 sts and work 40 rows in st-st.
Leave sts on spare needle.

bag

With 4mm(US 6) needles and A, cast on 90 sts and work 20 rows in st-st.
Foll chart working 1st–140th rows in st-st, ignoring elephant pocket.
Turn chart upside down and work 141st–180th rows.
181st row K27E, k36 sts from 1st row of elephant pocket chart, k27E.
182nd row P27E, p36 sts from 2nd row of elephant pocket chart, pp27E.
183rd–220th rows Work in st-st following chart.
221st row With A, k27, *p2, k2, rep from * 8 times, p2, k26.
222nd row P26, *k2, p2, rep from * 8 times, k2, p26.
223rd and 224th rows As 221st and 222nd rows.
225th row K27, cast/bind off 36 sts, k27.
226th row (place pocket) P27, p across 36 sts of pocket lining from spare needle, p27.
227th and 280th rows Work in st-st following chart.
Change to A and work 20 more rows in st-st.
Cast/bind off.

ties (make 2)

With 4mm(US 6) needles and B, cast on 5 sts and work 100cm(40in) in st-st.
Cast/bind off.

to finish

Weave in any loose ends. Slip stitch pocket lining into place. Fold end 20 rows in half and stitch down seams to the inside of the bag to make a casing for the ties. Fold bag in half RS facing and stitch side seams, leaving casing seams open. Thread ties through casing, left to right and right to left (see photograph). Sew the ends of each tie together to make a loop.

zoo toy bag chart

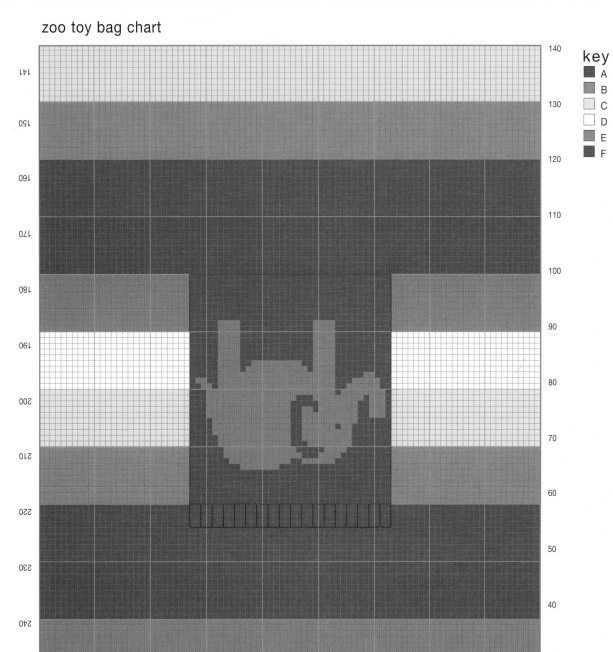

key
- A
- B
- C
- D
- E
- F

kaleidoscope throw

This design was inspired by memories of looking through a kaleidoscope as a child. The bold colours and retro feel will brighten any nursery and stimulate childrens' minds.

materials

5 50/1¾oz balls of Jaeger *Aqua Cotton* in main colour **M** (dark pink/India 322) and 4 balls in each of **A** (red/Ruby 316), **B** (orange/Marigold 331), **C** (yellow/Daffodil 330), **D** (purple/Comfrey 328), **E** (green/Herb 303) and **F** (blue/Blue Agate 317)

Pair each of 4mm(US 6) and 3¼mm(US 3) knitting needles

size

Approximately 94 x 94cm/37 x 37in
Each square 12.5 x 12.5cm/5 x 5in

tension/gauge

22 sts and 30 rows to 10cm/4in over st-st using 4mm(US 6) needles

abbreviations

alt alternate; **cm** centimetre(s); **foll(s)** follow(s)(ing); **in** inch(es); **k** knit; **mm** millimetre(s); **p** purl; **rep** repeat; **st(s)** stitch(es); **st-st** stocking/stockinette stitch

note

When working from chart, substitute different colours for colourways 2–7. Use separate small balls of yarn for each colour area and twist yarns at colour change to avoid holes.

basic square

With 4mm(US 6) needles and M, cast on 28 sts and work 38 rows in st-st foll chart.
Cast/bind off.
Make 25 squares beginning with a knit row and 24 squares beginning with a purl row.
make 7 squares in each of the 7 colourways.
Colourway 1 E, F, D, M, A, B.
Colourway 2 A, M, E, C, D, F.
Colourway 3 E, M, B, C, F, A.
Colourway 4 C, B, D, F, E, D.
Colourway 5 B, C, E, D, A, M.
Colourway 6 F, D, A, M, C, E.
Colourway 7 D, E, B, A, M, F.
centre section
To make centre section, stitch squares together in rows of 7, turning alternate squares 180 degrees. Make 4 rows (Rows 1, 3, 5 and 7) with the first square diagonal slanting to the right and 3 rows (Rows 2, 4 and 6) with the first diagonal slanting to the left. Join the rows together to make diamonds, see photograph.

edging

With 3¼mm(US 3) needles and M, cast on 195 sts.
1st–7th rows K1, p1, rep to last st, k1.
8th row Moss/seed 5 sts, cast/bind off 185 sts, moss/seed 5 sts.
On each set of 5 sts, work in moss/seed st until band fits side of blanket.
Next row Moss/seed 5 (band 1), cast on 185 sts, moss/seed 5 (band 2)
Work 7 rows in moss/seed st.
Cast/bind off.

to finish

Weave in loose ends. Stitch edging around centre section.

colourway 1 chart

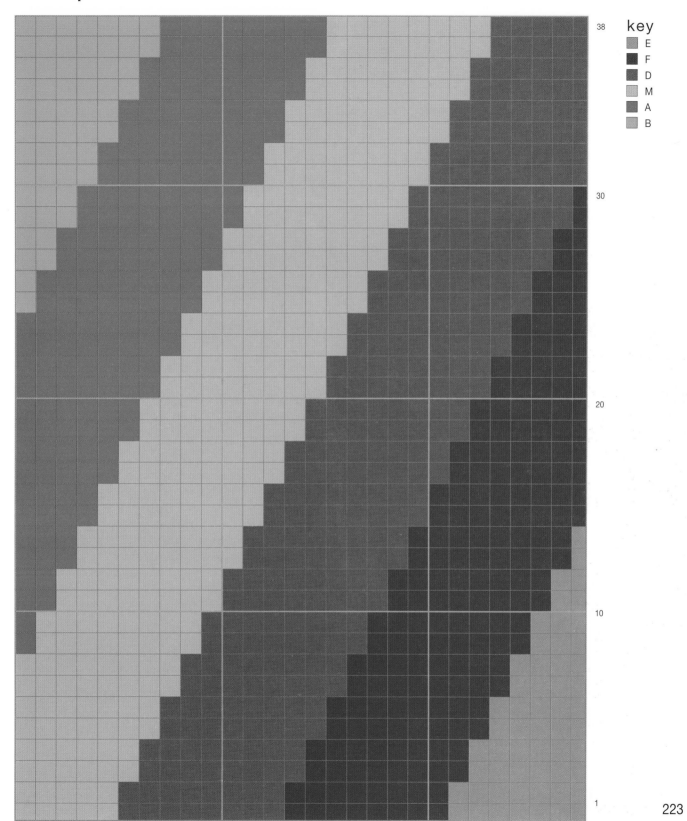

key
E
F
D
M
A
B

38

30

20

10

1

223

rainbow cushion

This colourful cushion will brighten up any nursery or bedroom and complements the Kaleidoscope Throw (see page 220).

materials

2 50g/1¾oz balls of Jaeger *Aqua Cotton* in main colour **M** (dark pink/India 322) and small amounts in each of **A** (red/Ruby 316), **B** (orange/Marigold 331), **C** (yellow/Daffodil 330), **D** (purple/Comfrey 328), **E** (green/Herb 303) and **F** (blue/Blue Agate 317)

Pair each of of 4mm(US 6) and 3¾mm(US 5) knitting needles

3 buttons

30 x 30cm/12 x 12in cushion pad

Size

30 x 30cm/12 x 12in

tension/gauge

22 sts and 30 rows to 10 cm/4in over st-st using 4mm(US 6) needles

abbreviations

cm centimetre(s); **in** inch(es); **k** knit; **k2tog** knit next 2 sts together; **mm** millimetre(s); **p** purl; **rep** repeat; **RS** right side; **st(s)** stitch(es); **st-st** stocking/stockinette stitch; **yo (yarn over needle)** take yarn over right needle to make a st

note

When working from chart, use separate small balls of yarn for each colour area and twist yarns at colour change to avoid holes.

to make

With 3¾mm(US 5) needles and M, cast on 66 sts

1st row *K1, p1, rep from * to end.

2nd row *P1, k1, rep from * to end.

Work 20cm/8in in moss/seed st.

Change to 4mm(US 6) needles and work 8 rows in moss/seed st.

9th row Moss/seed 5M, k 1st row of chart, moss/seed 5M.

10th row Moss/seed 5M, p 2nd row of chart, moss/seed 5M.

Cont to complete the 76-row colour chart in st-st while at the same time maintaining the moss/seed st borders in M.

Next row With M, moss/seed 5, k56, moss/seed 5.

Work 7 rows in moss/seed.

Change to 3¾mm(US 5) needles and work 19cm/7½in in moss/seed st.

Next row (buttonhole row) Moss/seed 16 (yo, k2tog, moss/seed 14) 3 times, moss/seed 2.

Work 3 more rows in moss/seed st.

Cast/bind off.

to finish

Fold cushion to make 30 x 30cm/12 x 12in front (RS facing) and sew side seams. (Note that the button holes are in correct position before sewing side seams.) This will give you a 10cm/4in overlap at centre back. Sew on buttons. Insert cushion pad.

rainbow cushion chart

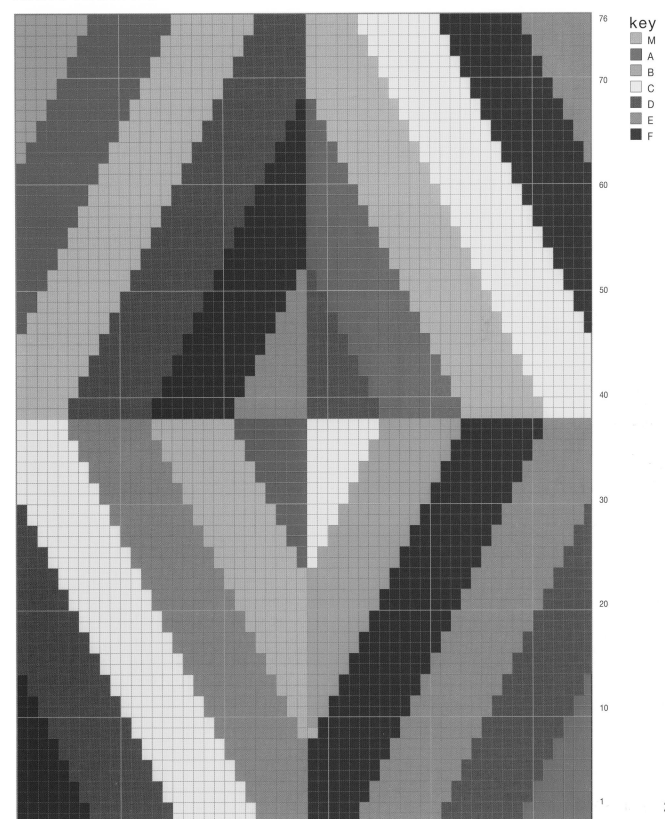

key
M
A
B
C
D
E
F

76
70
60
50
40
30
20
10
1

play cubes

These cubes are the perfect height for toddlers to sit on and have a useful side pocket for storing books and toys. They are fun and functional and can be stacked to save space.

materials

Green cube: 2 50g/1¾oz balls of Rowan *Handknit DK Cotton* in each of (pale green/Celery 309), (dark green/Slippery 316) and (blue/Galaxy 308)

Pink cube: 2 50g/1¾oz balls of Rowan *Handknit DK Cotton* in each of (pale pink/Sugar 303), (dark pink/Slick 313) and (red/Rosso 215)

Pair of 4mm(US 6) knitting needles

Washable filling

size

Each face of cube 30cm/12in square

tension/gauge

20 sts and 28 rows to 10cm/4in using st-st and 4mm(US 6) needles

abbreviations

cm centimetre(s); **foll(s)** follow(s)(ing); **in** inch(es); **k** knit; **mm** millimetre; **p** purl; **st(s)** stitch(es); **st-st** stocking/stockinette stitch

basic square

With 4mm(US 6) needles, cast on 60 sts and work 84 rows in st-st.
Cast/bind off.
Make 6 squares to make 1 cube.

patch pocket

With 4mm(US 6) needles, cast on 40 sts and work 55 rows in st-st.
56th row *k2, p2, rep from * to end.
Repeat 56th row 6 times more. (7 rows k2, p2 rib in all.)
Cast/bind off in k2, p2 rib.

green cube

Make 2 squares in dark green, 1 square each in light green and blue, 1 square working in stripes of 4 rows light green and 4 rows dark green and 1 square working in stripes of 4 rows blue and 4 rows dark green.
Work patch pocket in light green.

pink cube

Make 2 squares in dark pink, 1 square each in light pink and red, 1 square working in stripes of 4 rows light pink and 4 rows dark pink and 1 square working in stripes of 4 rows dark pink and 4 rows red.
Work patch pocket in red.

to finish

Sew patch pocket to a dark green or dark pink square. Join 6 squares together following the illustration below and leaving one seam open. Stuff cube with filling and close seam.

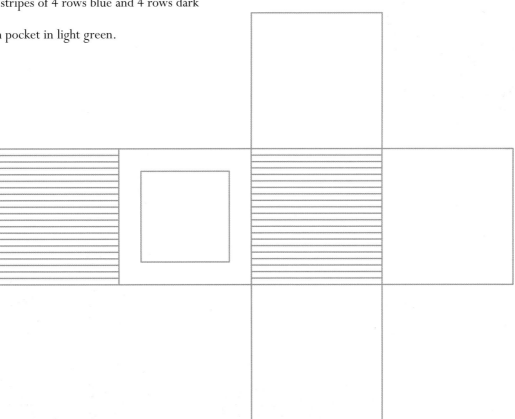

party flags

Perfect for birthday parties and special occasions, these flags are a great way to use up bits of leftover yarns. They are also a fun way to add colour to your child's nursery.

materials

Jaeger *Aqua Cotton* 15g each of two colours per flag: (yellow/Daffodil 330), (orange/Marigold 331), pale pink/Anemone 327), (dark pink/India 322), (red/Ruby 316), (purple/Comfrey 328), (green/Herb 303), (blue/Blue Agate 317), (dark blue/Deep 320)

Pair of 4mm(US 6) knitting needles

Cord, long enough to pass through all the flags and to make hanging loops at each end.

size

Each flag 20cm/8in long

tension/gauge

22 sts and 30 rows to 10cm/4in over st-st using 4mm(US 6) needles

abbreviations

cm centimetre(s); **dec** decreas(e)(ing); **foll(s)** follow(s)(ing); **in** inch(es); **k** knit; **k2tog** knit next 2 sts together; **mm** millimetre(s); **p** purl; **p2tog** purl next 2 sts together; **patt** pattern; **psso** pass slipped st over; **rem** remain(ing); **rep** repeat; **s1** slip next st; **skpo** s1, k1, psso; **st(s)** stitch(es); **st-st** stocking/stockinette stitch; **tbl** through back of loops; **WS** wrong side

notes

Work in st-st throughout, but k the first and last stitch on the p rows. When working from chart, use separate small balls of yarn for each colour area and twist yarns at colour change to avoid holes.

basic flag

With 4mm(US 6) needles, cast on 42 sts and work 10 rows.

11th row K2, skpo, k to last 4 sts, k2tog, k2.

12th–13th rows St-st.

14th row K1, p1, p2tog, p to last 4 sts, p2tog tbl, p1 k1.

15th–16th rows Work in st-st.

Rep 11th–16th rows until 6 sts rem. 64th row.

65th row K1, s1, k2tog, psso, k2.

66th–67th rows Work in st-st.

68th row K2tog, k2tog.

Cast/bind off.

to finish

Make a hem to thread cord through bunting by turning over first 4 rows to WS and stitching to back of flag. Weave in any loose ends.

striped flags

Work first 8 rows in A and then in stripe patt of 4 rows B, 4 rows A, repeating these last 8 rows throughout.

Flag 1 A orange, B dark pink

Flag 2 A green, B mid blue

Flag 3 A purple, B dark pink

Flag 4 A pale pink, B dark pink

Flag 5 A yellow, B green

spotted flags

Foll chart, remembering to work decs on 3rd and 4th stitches from edges.

Flag 1 A red, B orange

Flag 2 A dark pink, B pale pink

Flag 3 A dark blue, B pale blue

Flag 4 A green, B light blue

Flag 5 A orange, B yellow

spotted flag chart

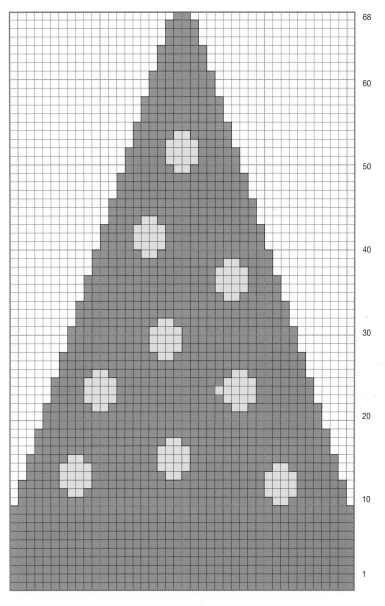

key

 A

☐ B

my own puppet theatre

This theatre is sure to keep little ones amused and entertained for hours. It can be hung at various heights for taller or shorter children and is easy to put up.

materials

3 50g/1¾oz balls of Rowan *Handknit DK Cotton* in **A** (yellow/Sunflower 304), 6 balls in **B** (blue/Galaxy 308), 3 balls in **C** (green/Gooseberry 219), 3 balls in **D** (red/Rosso 215), 1 ball in **E** (orange/Flame 254), and 2 balls in **F** (white/Ecru 251)

Small amounts of Rowan *Handknit DK Cotton* for head, hair and garments.

Oddments of Rowan *Handknit DK Cotton* to embroider eyes, mouth and nose

Pair of 4mm(US 6) knitting needles

Spare knitting needle

5.5m/18 feet tape, 4cm/1½in wide

60cm/24in hook and loop tape, 2cm/¾–1 in wide

1m/3 feet round wooden dowelling with 1.2cm/½in flat edge

size

Theatre: 81cm/32in wide and 137cm/54in long, plus edging

Glove puppets: 21.5cm/8½in tall

tension/gauge

20 sts and 28 rows to 10cm/4in over st-st using 4mm(US 6) needles

abbreviations

beg begin(ning); **cm** centimetre(s); **dec** decreas(e)(ing); **foll** follow(ing); **in** inch(es); **inc** increas(e)(ing); **k** knit; **p** purl; **RS** right side; **st(s)** stitch(es); **st-st** stocking/stockinette stitch; **WS** wrong side

note

When working from chart, use separate small balls of yarn for each colour area and twist yarns at colour change to avoid holes.

Break yarns and leave sts on spare needle.

Work 2nd set of 35 sts to match, foll chart 1. Do **not** break B.

Next row With B, k2, p33, cast on 89 sts, then working from sts on spare needle, p33, k2. 159 sts.

Work 1st–55th rows of chart 2 in st-st, keeping the k2 at the outer edges and working stars using the intarsia technique.

56th row K, to make a foldline.

Work 8 more rows in st-st.

Cast/bind off.

pointed edging

With 4mm(US 6) needles and B, cast 2 sts and work as follows.

1st row K2.

2nd row Inc in 1st st, k1. 3 sts.

3rd row K1, p1 inc in 3rd st. 4 sts.

4th row Inc in 1st st, k1, p1, k1. 5 sts.

5th–8th rows Cont in moss/seed st, inc at shaped edge on every row. 9 sts.

9th row Work in moss/seed st without shaping.

10th–16th rows Work in moss/seed st dec at shaped edge on every row, moss/seed st. 2 sts.

Repeat 1st–16th rows until straight edge fits along bottom of theatre.

Cast/bind off.

to make

With 4mm(US 6) needles and A, cast on 159 sts.

1st–4th rows K2, *p1, k1, rep from * to last 3 sts, p1 k2.

5th row K.

6th row K2, p to last 2 sts, k2.

7th–28th rows Rep 5th–6th rows 11 times.

29th row Change to B. K.

30th row With B, k2, p to last 2 sts, k2.

31st–56th rows Rep 29th–30th rows 13 times.

Cont in 28-row stripes, using C,D,E and then A,B and C until 27th row of the 2nd C stripe.

Next row K2, p31, k2, cast/bind off 89 sts, k2, p31, k2. On first set of 35 sts, work right side of stage.

Work 1st–97th rows of chart 1 in st-st, keeping k2 at the outer edges and working stars using intarsia technique.

curtains (make 2)

With 4mm(US 6) needles and D, cast on 85 sts.

1st–4th rows Work in moss st.

5th row K1, p1, k1, p1, k to last 4 sts, p1, k1, p1, k1.

6th row K1, p1, k1, p1, p to last 4 sts, p1, k1, p1, k1.

7th–8th rows As 5th and 6th rows.

****9th–16th rows** Change to F and repeat 5th–6th rows 4 times.

17th–24th rows Change to D and repeat 5th–6th rows 4 times.**

Repeat from ** to ** 3 times, then 9th–16th rows again.

Change to D and work 5th–8th rows, then work 1st–4th rows.

Cast/bind off in moss/seed st.

puppet theatre chart 1

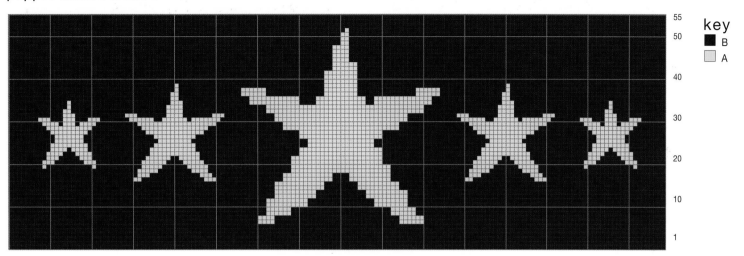

key
■ B
□ A

puppet theatre chart 2

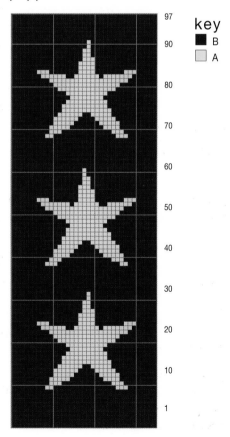

97
90
80
70
60
50
40
30
20
10
1

key
■ B
□ A

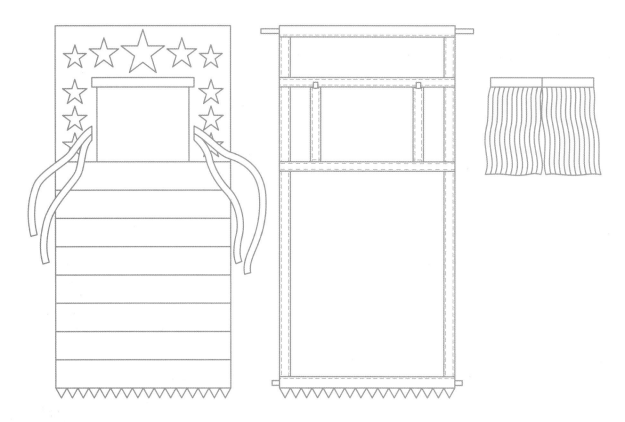

to finish

Weave in any loose ends. Fold top edge to WS at foldline and sew cast/bind off edge to WS of piece to make a casing to take dowelling for hanging. Sew tape across the WS of piece, level with top, bottom and sides of opening for re-enforcing with semi-circular dowelling. On each side of opening, fold a 122cm/48in length of tape in half and sew fold line one-third up on WS. Sew hook and loop tape across top of opening (on RS) and across one WS side edge of each of the curtains (stripes are vertical). Sew straight side of pointed edging to cast-on edge of theatre. Cut dowelling to size and insert into casings.

girl body (back and front alike)

With 4mm(US 6) needles and garment colour, cast on 32 sts and k 3 rows.
Change to contrasting colour and work 2 rows in st-st beg with a k row.
Change to garment colour, k 1 row and cont in st-st beg with a k row, dec 1 st each end of 1st and every foll 6th row to 22 sts. Cont in st-st until work measures 12cm/4¾in, ending with a k row.
K 3 rows.
Change to contrasting colour and work 2 rows in st-st.
Change to garment colour and cont in st-st until work measures 15cm/6in.
shape shoulders
Cast/bind off 5 sts at beg next 2 rows.
Cast/bind off

girl sleeves (both alike)

With 4mm(US 6) needles and garment colour, cast on 18 sts and k 3 rows.
Change to contrasting colour and work 2 rows in st-st beg with a k row.
Change to garment colour, k 1 row and then work 6 rows in st-st beg with a k row.
Cast/bind off.

girl head

With 4mm (US 6) needles and face colour, cast on 24 sts and work 2 rows in st-st.

3rd row *K2, inc, k1* to end. 30 sts.

4th–16th rows St-st.

shape top of head

17th row *K3, k2tog* to end.

18th row P.

19th row *K2, k2tog* to end.

20th row P.

21st row *K1, k2tog* to end.

22nd row *P2tog* to end.

Break yarn, leaving a long end and thread this through remaining sts. Pull sts together tightly and fasten securely. Join seam down to cast-on edge.

boy body

With 4mm (US 6) needles and garment colour, cast on 26 sts and k 3 rows.

Change to st-st and work 26 rows, dec 1st st at each end of 7th and 17th rows while at the same time maintaining the following stripe sequence:

Work 4 rows garment colour, then work 2 rows contrasting colour.

Work 6 rows garment colour, then work 2 rows contrasting colour.

These last 8 rows form the main stripe sequence.

27th row Cast on 4 sts, k to end.

28th row Cast on 4 sts, k2, p to last 2 sts, k2

29th–34th rows Work in st-st maintaining the stripe sequence and the k2 edges on all rows.

35th row K9, cast/bind off 12 sts, k9.

36th row K2, p7, cast on 12 sts, p7, k2.

37th–42nd rows Work in st-st maintaining the stripe sequence and the k2 edges on all rows.

43rd–44th rows Cast/bind off 4 sts, work to end.

45th–68th rows Work in st-st, inc 1 st at each end of 53rd and 63rd rows and maintaining stripe sequence.

69th–72nd rows K.

Cast/bind off.

boy head

Work as for Girl Head.

to finish

girl

Join shoulder seams of garment. Fold sleeves in half lengthways and pin to garment, centre of cast/bind-off edge to shoulder seam, and sew into place. Join side and underarm seams. Attach head to neck of garment, head seam to centre back.

Embroider facial features using darning needle. Add hair by cutting long strands of yarn and forming them into a bunch. Sew and secure the midpoint of the strands to the middle of the head, to cover the top and sides of the head but not the front or back. Sew and secure the bunches in position at the sides of the head.

boy

Join side and underarm seams. Attach head to neck of garment, head seam to centre back. Embroider facial features using darning needle. Add hair by cutting strands of long strands of yarn and forming them into a bunch. Sew and secure the midpoint of the strands to the middle of the head.

starlight blanket

Sleep under the stars in this snuggly cotton chenille baby blanket. The cosy yarn makes this a great blanket for newborns and those with delicate skins.

materials

8 50g/1¾oz balls of Rowan *Handknit DK Cotton* in main colour **M** (pale blue/Icewater 239) and 2 balls in **A** (dark blue/Galaxy 308)

1 50g/1¾oz balls of Rowan *Chunky Cotton Chenille* in **B** (ecru/Ecru 365)

Pair each 3¾mm(US 5) and 4mm (US 6) knitting needles

2 safety pins

size

Approximately 81x 76cm/32 x 30in

tension/gauge

20 sts and 28 rows to 10cm/4in over st-st using 4mm(US 6) needles

abbreviations

cm centimetre(s); **in** inch(es); **k** knit; **mm** millimetre(s); **p** purl; **rep** repeat; **st(s)** stitch(es); **st-st** stocking/stockinette stitch

note

When working from chart, use separate small balls of yarn for each colour area and twist yarns at colour change to avoid holes.

to make

With 3¾mm(US 5) needles and A, cast on 150 sts and
work 7 rows in moss/seed st.

1st row *K1, p1, rep from * to end.

2nd row *P1, k1, rep from * to end.

Work 5 more rows in moss/seed st as established.

8th row Place 5 sts on safety pin, with 4mm(US 6)
needles and M, k 140 sts from 1st row of chart, place
last 5 sts on safety pin.

On 140 sts, work 2nd–210th rows from chart using
intarsia method and st-st, starting with a p row. Leave
sts on needle.

edging

With 3¾mm(US 5) needles and A, rejoin yarn to one
set of 5 sts on safety pin.

Work in moss/seed st until band fits side of blanket.
Rep for other side.

Next row With RS facing and 3¾mm(US 5) needles
and A, moss/seed 5 sts from band, k across 140 sts of
blanket, moss/seed 5 sts from other band. 150 sts.

Work 7 rows in moss/seed st.

Cast/bind off.

to finish

Weave in any loose ends. Sew edgings to blanket sides.

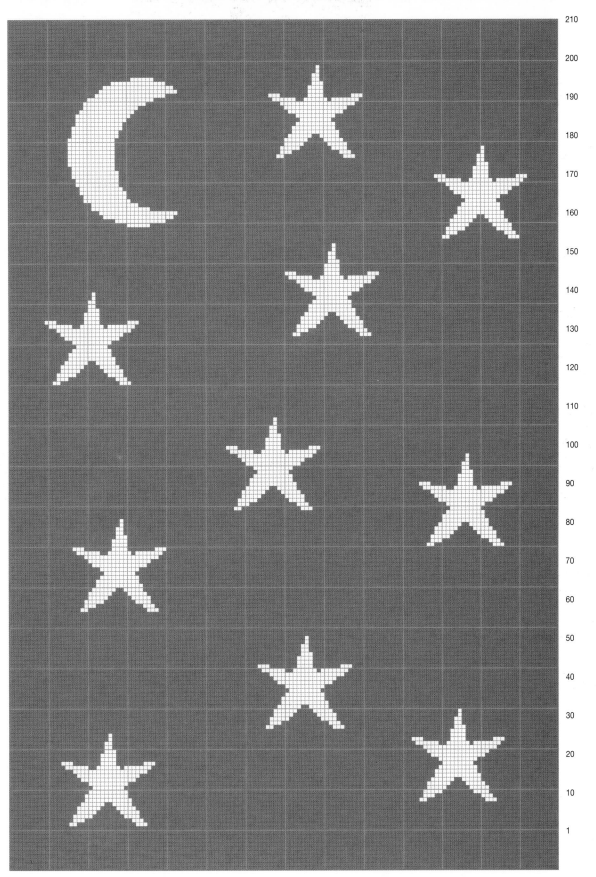

210
200
190
180
170
160
150
140
130
120
110
100
90
80
70
60
50
40
30
20
10
1

key

■ M
□ B

floating clouds cushion

Ideal for the nursery, this soft, woolly cloud cushion will be
a favourite with all little daydreamers. The pretty buttoned
fastening on the back makes it easy to clean, too.

materials

4 50g/1¾oz balls of Rowan *Kid
Classic* in main colour **M**
(blue/Merry 818) and 2 balls in
A (ecru/Feather 828)
Pair of 5½mm(US 9) knitting
needles
4 buttons
36 x 36cm/14½ x 14½in cushion pad

size

36 x 36cm/14½ x 14½in

tension/gauge

19 sts x 25 rows to 10cm/4in over
st-st using 5½mm(US 9) needles

abbreviations

cm centimetre(s); **cont** continue;
in inch(es); **k** knit; **mm**
millimetre(s); **PM** place marker; **p**
purl; **rep** repeat; **RS** right side;
st(s) stitch(es); **st-st** stocking/
stockinette stitch

note

When working from chart, use separate small
balls of yarn for each colour area and twist
yarns at colour change to avoid holes.

to make

Starting with the overlap, with 5½mm(US 9) needles and M, cast on 67 sts.

Work in moss/seed st as follows:

1st–2nd rows *K1, p1, rep from * to last st, k1.

3rd row (buttonhole row) Moss/seed 4 sts, *cast/bind off 2 sts, moss/seed 17 sts, rep from * twice more, cast/bind off 2 sts, moss/seed 4 sts.

4th row Moss/seed 4 sts, *cast on 2 sts, moss/seed 17 sts, rep from * twice more, cast on 2 sts, moss/seed 4 sts.

5th–6th rows Moss/seed st.

Change to st-st and work 45 rows, PM at each end of 39th row for foldline.

46th–166th rows Cont in st-st and using intarsia technique, work from chart, PM at each end of 124th row for foldline. Work 10 rows st st.

Work 14 rows in moss/seed st.

Cast/bind off.

to finish

Weave in loose ends. Fold at markers, RS together, making sure that at the overlap the buttonholes are in the middle of the 'sandwich'. Sew the side seams. Turn RS out. Sew on buttons. Insert cushion pad.

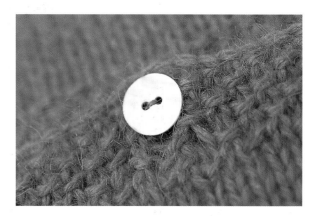

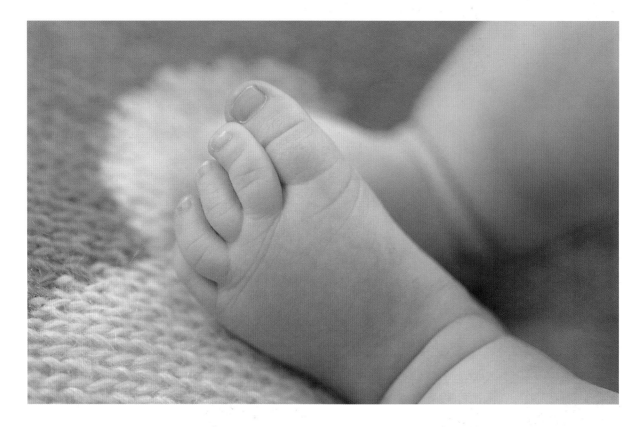

clouds motif

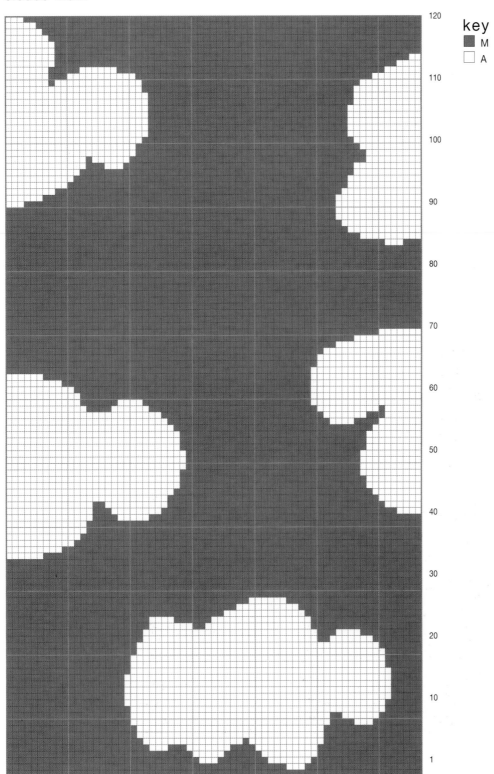

useful information

knitting abbreviations

The following are the general abbreviations used in the patterns. Special abbreviations are given with the individual patterns.

alt alternate
beg begin(ning)
cm centimetre(s)
cont continu(e)(ing)
cont straight continu(e)(ing) without shaping
dec decreas(e)(ing)
foll follow(s)(ing)
g gram(s)
g-st gram(s)
in inch(es)
inc increas(e)(ing)
k knit
kfb k into front and back of next st to inc one st
kp knit then purl into next st
m metre(s)
m1 make one st by picking up and working into back of loop between last st and next st
mm millimetre(s)
oz ounce(s)
p purl
patt pattern
pfb p into front and back of next st to inc one st
pk purl then knit into next st
psso pass slipped stitch over

rem remain(s)(ing)
rep repeat(s)(ing)
RS right side
skpo slip 1, k1, pass slipped st over
sk2togpo slip 1, k2tog, pass slipped st over
sl slip
ssk slip 1 knitwise, slip 1 knitwise, insert tip of left needle into fronts of 2 slipped sts and k2tog tbl
st(s) stitch(es)
st-st stocking/stockinette stitch
tbl through back of loop(s)
tog together
WS wrong side
yd yard(s)
yf yarn forward – bring yarn forward between needles and over right needle to make a st
yo (yon) yarn over needle – take yarn over right needle to make a st
yrn yarn round needle – wrap yarn around right needle from front to back and bring it to front again between needles to make a st
* repeat instructions after asterisk or between asterisks as many times as instructed
[ ] repeat instructions inside [ ]s as many times as instructed

substituting yarns

Knitting patterns always specify a particular brand of yarn. If you decide to use an alternative yarn be sure to calculate the number of balls or hanks you need by the metre (yard) rather than by the yarn weight. If you want to use a different yarn to the one suggested then match the shade as closely as possible.

yarn conversion chart

To convert	multiply by
grams to ounces	0.0352
ounces to grams	28.35
centimetres to inches	0.3937
inches to centimetres	2.54
metres to yards	0.9144
yards to metres	1.0936

UK and US knitting terminology

Most terms used in UK and US knitting patterns are the same, but a few are different. Where terms are different, they appear in the instructions divided by a /.

UK	US
cast off	bind off
moss stitch	seed stitch
stocking stitch	stockinette stitch
tension (size of stitch)	gauge
yarn over needle	yarn over (yo)
yarn forward	yarn over (yo)
yarn round needle	yarn over (yo)

suppliers

Rowan Yarns
Green Lane Mill, Holmfirth
West Yorkshire, HD7 1RW
01484 681881
www.rowanyarns.co.uk

Jaeger Yarns
As Rowan
01484 680050

knitting needle conversion chart

This chart shows you how the different knitting needle-size systems compare.

Metric	US sizes	Old UK
2mm	0	14
2¼mm	1	13
2¾mm	2	12
3mm		11
3¼mm	3	10
3¾mm	5	9
4mm	6	8
4½mm	7	7
5mm	8	6
5½mm	9	5
6mm	10	4
6½mm	10½	3
7mm	10½	2
7½mm	11	1
8mm	11	0
9mm	13	00
10mm	15	000

index

acknowledgements

publisher acknowledgements

The Publishers would like to thank William Bentley Archer, Daniel Attwood, Louis Barnes-Jones, Charlotte Barton, Lily Belle de la Mer, Charlotte Brown, Olivia Campbell, Daisy Carville, Maysoon Collier, Natalie d'Enno, Olivia Dornan, Hannah Goodman, Owen Harris, Rumi Hugo-Fox, Emily Merrit Moore, Lola Perrin, Tom Proctor, Ryan Sparham-O'Reilly, Jack Swainston, Neo Tanner, Minnie Venning, Lola Walters, Kitty Wynne-Mellor, Toby Wynne-Mellor and Mason Young for being such wonderful models. They would also like to thank Jehane Boden Spiers, Gordon and Sheila Pope, and Zoë Mellor for the kind loan of their homes. Thanks also to Alex Owen for helping with the children, the Bluebird Café in Goring, the flower stall in Hove, Hannah Goodman, Emma Hancox and Emily Wilkinson.

Executive Editor Katy Denny
Managing Editor Clare Churly
Pattern Checkers Rosy Tucker and Pauline Hornsby
Executive Art Editor Tim Pattinson
Designers Maggie Town and Beverly Price, one2six creative
Photographer Adrian Pope
Illustrator Kuo Kang Chen
Senior Production Controller Manjit Sihra